Talks with Emanuel Hurwitz

By the same author

Beyond the Music Lesson
Between Music Lessons

For Kay,
with affection and admiration.

A photo from the early 1950s

Talks with Emanuel Hurwitz

82 years with the violin

RIKI GERARDY

Zelia
2006

First published in 2006 by
Zelia Ltd.
78 Wolmer Gdns.
Edgware
HA8 8QD

ISBN-10: 0–9544675–2–3
ISBN-13: 978–0–9544675–2–4

A CIP catalogue record for this book is available from
the British Library

Typeset in 11/13pt Sabon by
Cambrian Typesetters, Camberley, Surrey
Printed in Great Britain by Halstan, Amersham, Bucks.

Table of Contents

THE KNACKS OF TALENT

GREAT VIOLINISTS

List of Illustrations

Preface

Emanuel Hurwitz CBE, universally known as Manny, is now eighty-seven and still a constant source of musical wisdom. His perceptive comments can be surprising: he tends not to state the obvious, often being a couple of steps ahead in thought. Usually the subject is further illuminated by an anecdote chosen from an apparently endless collection.

Manny says that the circus band is perhaps the only type of group he hasn't played in. He has performed as soloist, in duo recitals, in the London String Trio and Piano Quartet, the Hurwitz String Quartet, the Aeolian String Quartet and the Melos Ensemble. He has led the Boyd Neel Orchestra, the Jacques Orchestra, the Goldsborough Orchestra—known later as the English Chamber Orchestra and the Philharmonia Orchestra. He has taught at the Royal Academy of Music, the Royal Scottish Academy and in chamber music courses worldwide. He still adjudicates in major competitions, teaches privately and is widely known as an accessible personality, always willing to dispense good advice.

Chamber music, rather than solo playing, was always Manny's first interest. Such a career tends to be about musical values rather than self-promotion. This has always been apparent in his music making, and in his assessment of the great musicians he worked with.

Our contact began through a family connection. My father's sister, who died before I was born, was one of Manny's first teachers. As a schoolboy, I first heard him play in the Melos Ensemble. More recently, inspiration for the present volume came from his helpful suggestions when I was completing my first book, **Beyond the Music Lesson.**

We had started by discussing the difference in technical and musical requirements between concerto and sonata playing—the expansion of virtuosity into a wider musicality. Finding his ideas immensely clear and practical, I realised that they should be written down.

In this book, these ideas, together with other important aspects of violin technique, are preceded by an account of Manny's colourful life, to show the context within which his musical philosophy developed. Also, there is an appreciation of the great solo violinists with whom he worked or heard in concert. He has always taken the keenest interest in their recordings, partly for the great help they can offer young players in developing style and individuality.

This book is in Manny's own words—all my questions and comments are in italics. It has been compiled and edited from a number of conversations recorded at the beginning of 2003, and from many further discussions since that time.

I would like to thank Douglas Rogers and Anne Martin for their generous help with the final editing, and Tully Potter for kindly contributing several photos.

R.G. 2006

My Life

Aged eighteen months with my parents

1

. . . .

Family

How good is your memory of past events? Many of my old friends, over the years, have reminded me of occasions on which we've played together in various places . . . it's only after they've mentioned it that I begin to have some vague recollection. Of all the concerts I have played in, it is amazing how many I have totally forgotten, although there is a large collection of programmes upstairs. I realise that there are only particular pieces of music, and certain players, that have really impinged on my consciousness.

Bizarre memories come back of my travels . . . relaxing in a square in Caracas, Venezuela, with an aperitif, wondering about the banging noises; then my colleague returning from checking out a restaurant saying 'Not that one—there are two guys inside shooting at each other!' . . . travelling from Moscow to what was Leningrad, in a real old-style luxury railway carriage complete with large samovars; not so much aware of my Russian ancestry as feeling that, if I lived there, I would probably be in jail as a dissident . . .

How far back does your Russian connection go—how many generations? My father, who was born in England, was the son of a refugee who in 1880 came from Vilnius, in Lithuania, the town where Jascha Heifetz was born. *So you are not totally English, although born in England?* Not by blood, but by temperament I am a genuine Englishman. Somebody who would be reading the Times in the first-class carriage of a train, choosing to ignore the fact that a murder was taking place in the corridor. I was brought up to be an English gentleman.

My mother was born in Russia, in Ekaterinaslav, somewhere near Minsk; her family name was Gabrilowitsch. She told me about life in Russia; how, during the pogroms, the family would go down to the cellar when the Cossacks rode in. At the age of nine she came to England with her parents and several brothers and sisters. While travelling through Germany, her parents, not having passports for all the children, gave her baby sister some diluted vodka to drink, to be

With my mother and my father's parents

sure she would be sleeping as they went through the control. England was only considered a staging point, but they decided to stay for a while. Most of the family went on to the USA around 1914. When they reached Ellis Island, the immigration official said to them 'Take a bath and drop the itch', so they became Gabriel. My mother didn't go with them, because by then she had met my father.

What was your father's work? My parents met while working for the same firm of tobacconists, run by a family of four or five brothers called Slowe, a comfortable Anglicisation of the name Slobodinski. My mother was rolling handmade Russian and Turkish-style cigarettes; my father was doing the firm's books, being a twenty-year-old accountant—quite a wizard mathematically, who never even dreamt of getting a degree. The idea of going to a university was totally outside the possibilities of his lifestyle. *Was he qualified as an accountant?* No, not at all—he just had a natural talent for this work.

Where were you born? In Aldgate, on May 7th 1919—nearly a Cockney, but not quite. This was the day of the Treaty of Versailles, the administrative conclusion of the First World War. It was also the year of the Spanish Flu epidemic in which millions perished worldwide—one of my uncles was a victim of it.

It was the end of a decade that had begun in the Edwardian era and saw the disintegration of the old world order. Debussy and Renoir both died the year before I was born: for me Debussy seemed a tragic figure, as he had died while only half-way through his series of six instrumental sonatas.

In my early years I loved hearing stories about the war from my uncle Sid, who had been invalided out before the conflict ended, and from my father who, however, had not been accepted for military service as he was only five feet one in height.

Did you have a happy family life in those days? Very much so: to balance a Russian Jewish mother who was a touch hysterical, I had a father who was consoling and conciliating. My mother was incredibly kind and very proud of me. I loved her cooking and liked going with her on shopping trips. Somehow she never learned how to write in English. I remember how she wrote from right to left across the

Aged five

page when she wrote letters to her family in Yiddish. Her family, though not religious, were observant people; her parents remained orthodox but she became liberal. By contrast, my father was from a free-thinking family. He would impress on me that our visits to the Synagogue on high and holy days were only made for the sake of my mother.

2

. . . .

Violin Lessons

I was given a violin outfit on my fifth birthday and I remember distinctly my first lesson: it was at school and the teacher's fee was sixpence. *What made your mother give you a violin?* I think she had decided that it was the correct thing for a young Jewish boy—it was as simple as that. *Were either of your parents musical?* They didn't play any instrument, but loved music and always encouraged me.

My first teacher was a lady called Hilda Morris who taught locally; I learned with her for two years. *Were you well started on the violin?* I have no recollection of anything that lady taught me, but remember my first attempt to tune the quarter-size violin. Since I could not turn the pegs, I laid the instrument on a chair and put my knee on the fingerboard. To my surprise, the neck of the violin came out! Fortunately, it came out cleanly and was repaired quite easily.

Did subsequent teachers have to take you back to the beginning, to change your technique? No, because I played very naturally.

My sister Lillian was born when I was six. This was good news for me, as it meant that my mother had lots of other things to keep her busy. Lillian was quite a shy child: while I was fairly precocious, she was happy to remain in the background. We were friendly, but the difference in our ages decreased the chances of intimacy.

At my first school, being Jewish meant being allowed to kick a ball around in the playground instead of attending prayers. My next school, King Edwards, was situated near a Catholic School, which brought me invitations from boys there to join them in fights against the Protestants, or vice versa.

At the age of eight I went for violin lessons to Leon Bergman, who I liked very much. He had taught a lot of the East End Jewish boys, including the great Albert Sandler, who became king of the light music world, and his brother Harold, who made his career in America. Albert was a fine violinist. One evening, my father took me to dinner at the well-known restaurant where he played, so that we could hear him. At one point in the evening he rattled off the last movement of the Mendelssohn Concerto, just for fun.

The study books I was given at that time had all the usual little tunes. *Did you learn much from Bergman?* I was told, all the time, to try to listen to myself playing. Also, to play in tune and to use good legato bow strokes. I remember the first book by Emil Kreuz, in which each couple of pages had another scale and a new position to learn. It had directions for playing with the whole bow, or at the middle, point or nut—I very much enjoyed doing those things. I had to prepare a different scale each week. Occasionally, if my teacher felt that my right wrist was stiff, he would tap it with his bow.

After the lessons, my mother would give us a cup of tea and a biscuit, and we would listen together to a Heifetz recording. I had two of these: the **Ronde des Lutins** by Bazzini, and Wieniawski's **Scherzo Tarantelle**. Bergman would exclaim 'Ah, Jascha, what a left hand . . . but what a fantastic right arm!'—he had been a fellow pupil of Jascha Heifetz in Leopold Auer's class. He also liked Mischa Elman, and we would sometimes play his recording of Massenet's **Meditation** from **Thais**.

I was very fortunate in that I was taken to lots of concerts from the age of eight. *What was the first that you remember going to?* The Workers' Circle held six o'clock Sunday concerts somewhere in the City. Later they were renamed the South Place Concerts. I can recall my father taking me to a violin recital there. He wanted me to hear some Paganini caprices that were on the programme. I distinctly remember being in the hall where a young man played with great brilliance; he looked quite formal and dapper. This was William Primrose—before he became a viola player. *What was your impression of the Paganini caprices?* Well, at my age they were like magic. As a small boy, I never dreamt or even thought of trying to play those pieces.

For Fritz Kreisler's concerts, we always had good seats at the front of the Queen's Hall so that I was able to hear and watch him at close quarters.

When I was nine, the Jewish Chronicle held a music festival and I was put into the youngest category, the Under-Thirteen. I played a charming little piece written by Ludwig Lebell, a cello teacher at the Royal College of Music. All these years later I can still remember the first few bars . . . The adjudicator regretted that I had not waited for the four bars of piano introduction before beginning. Strangely enough, I had only once heard the piano part before I played in the competition. However, he said that I played very well and I was declared the winner.

At this competition I was still playing on a three-quarter size violin. Although I wasn't a particularly big boy, I had very long arms. So, when I was ten, my teacher took me to find a full-size violin which I would soon be needing. We went to a well-known violin shop in Moorgate that was frequented by lots of the silent film string players, who would often pop in for strings and accessories. The owner, Isadore Caplan, was blind, but seemed to know where everything was in his shop and would go unerringly to it.

We spent the whole of a Sunday morning there, during which I tried four violins. My teacher approved my choice, which was a three-year-old Collin-Mezin junior. I was absolutely drunk with the power of this violin, a strong mezzo-soprano sound. I remember that it cost £8, and another 15 shillings (75p) for the case, bow, rosin, pitch pipe and spare strings. There were gold decorations on the pegs, and they didn't stick, as had those of my three-quarter violin.

Aged ten, trying my full-size violin, although I was to play the 3/4 for a few months more

My mother was very supportive and always took me to the violin competitions I entered. However, life with her was unpredictable, in that I never knew if I would be praised or screamed at. Whenever she thought I hadn't done enough practice she became hysterical. She would curl up a plait in each hand and bang her head against the wall a few times, screaming that I was the son of the devil, before collapsing into a chair and sighing 'Oi veh!'. It happened about twice a week and was carefully timed to coincide with my father's return from work. Fortunately, my father was more phlegmatic and knew how to keep the peace. He was affectionate, but not demonstrative. In the evenings he would do his accounts quite effortlessly, whilst listening to a symphony on the radio.

The world changed considerably in the Twenties. The younger generation, once returned from the war, questioned the values of their elders. Women now had the vote and moral attitudes changed. All around the world this was a time of economic expansion. *Have you many memories of this decade?* I remember the excitement of going to the first talking picture, Al Jolson's **The Jazz Singer**, also **Showboat** in which Paul Robeson sang **Ol' Man River**. I saw a massive airship—it might have been the R101, which later crashed in France. When I was nine my father bought a radio. There was a lot of talk in those times about the troubles in Germany, also about the discovery of the tomb of Tutankhamun, and whether those who disturbed it might be cursed. However, it appears that most of them lived reasonably long lives!

3

Growing Up

We lived in a large house, on three floors. There was a small self-contained flat which was usually rented out. When I was twelve our uncle Michael came to live with us for a while. He was a benevolent white magician and a well-known author, often writing in the papers under his pseudonym, Michael Juste. He had a successful bookstore in Museum Street called Atlantis; however I was rather sceptical when he used to talk about things like reincarnation.

I remember also my paternal grandfather, who liked me to play Jewish tunes for him, particularly klezmer music. Yet he didn't want me to take my playing too seriously, in case I actually became a klezmer—the name for a traditional Jewish musician of Eastern Europe. This, he thought, would be rather low-class.

My secondary education was at Clarks College: the school was a rival to Pitmans, of shorthand fame, and had its own version of this. I went there from twelve to fourteen, so did not have to begin learning shorthand—that discipline only started at fifteen. However, we were given early pre-secretarial assignments, in the form of letters in handwriting that was difficult to read; our task was to decipher them and make fair copies. Paper was expensive and cost us tuppence for each double foolscap sheet. The school day began with mathematics, with a column of a dozen five figure numbers to add up in double-quick time. I always went to a private, rather than a state school, because of my need for time off to practise, which was done mainly in those periods devoted to football, cricket or swimming. It was rather distressing not to be able to take part in these activities that I really enjoyed. *What were you like academically, at school?* I was pretty bright. When I decided to leave, at fourteen, the headmaster was rather sorry that I had chosen such a 'dubious' career as music.

Did you read a lot? I was an avid reader of all the main childrens' books of those days. I particularly liked the books of Edith Nesbitt; they are still in print and I am very pleased that my children and grandchildren have been able to read them. When twelve or thirteen I read anything I could possibly find by H. Rider Haggard—the wonderful, romantic **King Solomon's Mines** type of stories, also Jules Verne. Later, Conan Doyle and P.G.Wodehouse, followed by George Elliot and Tobias Smollet, Dickens, Wilkie Collins and also science fiction.

Your aunt, Gladys Chester, was my third violin teacher when I was about twelve. *I never knew her, because she died three years before I was born. My family ran a small music school in their house, on the corner of Bethune Road, in Stamford Hill.* We lived in Bethune Road for about twelve years. *What are your memories of my aunt and of the school?* I don't remember being taught any specific technique. Every few weeks I would be given a new study and another piece of music to learn. What I remember most is playing string quartets. I also used to go once a week to play chamber music after school from about five o'clock onwards. The school's outstanding pupil was called Ruth Pearl; she later moved to Australia and made a fine career.

Was Yehudi Menuhin known in your part of the world? Yes, but I didn't know of him until he was twelve—he made his first recording when he came to England. My father bought me a ten inch record of his when I was nine: the **Allegro** by Fiocco and **La Capriccieuse** by Reis. My mother said to me 'He sounds better than you!' I replied 'He's three years older!' Actually, I was very modest and, although I felt that I couldn't possibly do as well, I very much enjoyed my playing.

Why did you change teacher again after a year? My father had several friends who were string players working in cinemas. One of them thought I wasn't learning anything specific, but was just playing in various pupils' concerts. He said I ought to go to some big fiddle player to be pushed, and recommended his own teacher, Norbert Wethmar, a big virtuoso and leader of the Gershom Parkinton Quintet, which was on the radio every week.

I liked Wethmar straight away, and even more when he played to me. I found it very exciting to be in a room beside somebody making a sound like that. He came from Brussels, and had studied with Massart, winning the Grand Prix both there and, a year later, at the Paris Conservatoire. He had one of those iron-clad techniques—not great subtlety but incredible technical efficiency. *Did he push you in that direction?* He tried to, yes. I was thirteen when I went to him and, straight away, he made me learn the first Bach Solo Sonata in G minor, which was quite a lot harder than anything I had played before. Occasionally we listened to some of his records, made for Regal

Zonophone. He was one of the top 'session' fiddle players for light music in those days—the others were Alfredo Campoli and Albert Sandler. Whereas Wethmar had a virtuoso vibrato that was fast and close, Campoli was an entirely different sort of player: he had a warm, round sound, using a fairly wide vibrato that made him seem perhaps a little too schmaltzy. My own vibrato happened to be rather wobbly when I was young. In fact I remember my teacher saying 'Bah, you sound like Campoli!' *So what did Wethmar teach you about vibrato?* He didn't give me any idea of how to get a vibrato like his.

When I was fourteen, I was lent a violin made by Nicholas Aine, another Mirecourt maker. It was one of a number that had been reduced in size by the firm of W.E.Hill & Sons. Wethmar played on a marvellous sounding violin by George Kloz, which he played with a strong 62 gram Lamy bow. One day, during my lesson, his wife opened the door of his study to bring him a cup of coffee. The door knocked the bow out of his hand and into the fireplace, splitting the frog. He was very unhappy about this. One day, he told me that he was soon going to Paris, so he would ask Monsieur Lamy to make him another frog. On his return, I asked him if the bow had been repaired. He told me that Lamy, being too busy at the time, had sent him to his younger colleague, Eugene Sartory, who worked four doors away. Sartory's bows are now even more sought after than those of Lamy.

Another memory is of Wethmar deciding that he would like to panel a wall of his small library with cedar wood. My father proceeded to bring him along bags of cigar boxes. They were pulled apart and the pieces fixed in place on the wall.

My lessons with him went on for about a year and then, at fourteen, I won a scholarship to the Royal Academy of Music. I had a choice: whether to go on with school or to take up this scholarship. Music was something pleasurable and easy, so I immediately chose that direction. *How did you feel about leaving school?* Wonderful. *When did you first think that music might be your life?* The choice was automatic from the age of fourteen—I just expected it. By then I was doing occasional jobs, modestly paid, in local orchestras and opera companies. Asked to lead the second violin section in an amateur performance of Traviata, for a fee of two shillings, I noticed that if I didn't come in the others in the section didn't either. During the interval I complained and asked for a higher fee because of my responsibilities: I was given another sixpence.

4

. . . .

Life in the Thirties

The world changed again at the beginning of the Thirties, after the United States stock market crash late in 1929. The widespread repercussions were to some extent connected with the repayment of debts from the war a decade earlier: this was a time of high unemployment. *What do you remember about life in the Thirties?* Reading about the discovery of the planet Pluto, reported on the front page of the Daily Herald, which also had an account of the first World Cup. There was excitement about the new transatlantic liner, the Queen Mary, and concern about the destruction of the Crystal Palace in a fire. I remember my father buying a copy of Aldous Huxley's notorious new book, Brave New World.

How much did you notice changes around you at the beginning of the depression? I just sailed through life perfectly happily as a music student, only interested in playing my violin and occasionally going down to see Tottenham Hotspur play on Saturdays. I liked reading, playing table tennis, going to the youth club and taking long walks. People within our circle were certainly not deprived.

Three fine composers, Delius, Holst and Elgar, died in 1934. This was not long after Menuhin had performed and recorded with Elgar his Violin Concerto; my father bought these records with a small group of three friends. They cost £1 16 shillings, virtually half a week's wage, so the group used to share recordings that they bought together. In 1935 the Silver Jubilee of George V was celebrated, but he died soon after. Then followed the scandal of the abdication of his son, after only nine months. I remember reading about it in various newspapers, but any feelings just passed me by. We took it as an expected thing that there would be a different king. His brother, who became George VI, didn't really want the throne but had to manage, somehow or other. He was a very shy man with a slight stammer.

While my parents never had an enormous income, they managed to live comfortably. My father's salary was unfortunately supplemented by two hundred free cigarettes a week. He was a heavy smoker who died in 1954 at the age of sixty-one. When I started smoking at fourteen, my parents didn't like it at all. Right up until the 1930s the adverts claimed that smoking was beneficial—good for the nervous system and helpful against germs. In certain schools in South Africa, at the beginning of the twentieth century, it was obligatory for schoolboys to smoke, because it was considered to be calming for the nerves. Nearly all the soldiers smoked while in the trenches during the First World War. Many doctors knew it was unhealthy, but they hardly wished to deny this pleasure to those that might be about to die. A little book, written by a doctor in 1924, gave ideas on how to be healthy; it advised against smoking. On reaching the age of sixty-one I gave up the habit.

Did your family have sufficient money to weather the depression? It wasn't easy, because my father had made the unfortunate mistake of going into business for himself—just six months before the depression started. *As an accountant?* No, as a cigarette and confectionary seller: he leased a couple of kiosks in railway stations. *What happened to this business?* It collapsed, and it took him about ten years to pay off the debts. *Was your life in any way affected by this?* Well, his life was. From the time I was fifteen, he found it very difficult to support me. Most of my musical friends went into the family business on reaching the age of fourteen. One very talented fellow pupil stopped his lessons and joined his father in the fur trade. To help me pursue my studies, my father obtained help from a society called **Jewish Education Aid Assistance**, formed by a group of amiable, reasonably wealthy ladies, who donated money towards such projects. They contributed £100 a year for three years.

My father bought a second house in 1935, when I was about sixteen, managing to keep the first one by renting it out. *How did the timing of that purchase go with his unfortunate change of business?* It was about two years into that change—he never left his original job. *I thought you meant that he burned his boats.* Not by any means, he had money coming in. The tobacco firm he worked for was called Leon—they must have had sixty or seventy small tobacco shops around London. They sold pipes and Dunhill lighters; they also had a range of hosiery shops called Noel Brothers—which was Leon backwards. *What happened to that business in subsequent years?* After my father died I had no further contact with these people. There was still a modest mortgage on the house which they paid, along with a small pension for my mother, who lived until 1967.

In 1936 there came the unexpected news of the death of a great-uncle, of whose existence I was totally ignorant. He had been a very important pianist and conductor in America. Although my mother's family was not orthodox they didn't acknowledge his existence, because he had committed the unspeakable sins of marrying out of the faith and giving concerts on the Sabbath. His name was Ossip Gabrilowitsch, and his frowned-upon marriage, in 1909, was to Clara Clemens, Mark Twain's daughter. A distinguished pianist, he also became conductor of the Detroit Symphony Orchestra. I have a solo recording of his, which includes the Schumann Piano Quintet with the Flonzaley Quartet. Albert Spalding, in his memoirs, spoke of his very gentle personality.

My great uncle, Ossip Gabrilowitch
(Courtesy Tully Potter Collection)

THÉATRE DE L'ALHAMBRA

Concerts Ysaye

Quinzième année

DIMANCHE 12 FÉVRIER 1911, à 2 1/2 heures

QUATRIÈME CONCERT D'ABONNEMENT

sous la direction de Monsieur

EUGÈNE YSAŸE

ET AVEC LE CONCOURS DE MONSIEUR

OSSIP GABRILOWITSCH

PIANISTE

A concert featuring my great uncle

In some circles, attitudes can mellow with time. I have been very happily married to my wife, Kay, for fifty-eight years and have had an active playing career, which often meant playing every day of the week—life choices identical to those of my great uncle. However, I have been more fortunate than him, in not having been ostracised within the family circle. Anyway, he seems to have survived pretty well without us!

5

Royal Academy of Music

Can you remember anything about the day of your audition for the scholarship? There were seven or eight of us, all aged fourteen, competing for two scholarships given by Bronislaw Huberman. I performed the Bach A minor Concerto, not being particularly advanced at that time. Huberman, who had a very pronounced squint, just sat there. The first scholarship was given to a boy called Anthony English, who played the Mendelssohn Concerto, so he was definitely ahead of me—but I won the second one. A different scholarship went to one Aubrey Appleton who, in 1936, gave an excellent performance of the Walton Viola Concerto, not long after Frederick Riddle had premiered it. It was included in our annual concert with Sir Henry Wood, at the Queen's Hall.

Was the Royal Academy in its present building in Marylebone Road when you first attended? Yes, it had been there since 1924. My teacher was Sidney Robjohns. He was an excellent teacher of young people and I learned a great deal from him. He taught me to learn to listen to myself, to change position cleanly and accurately, and to play in tune: also to play into the string, so as to produce a real sound from the violin. *Did he illustrate what he wanted?* Yes, he had a good, firm sound, but his playing didn't excite me. He had stopped giving concerts in his twenties. Many famous teachers, including Ivan Galamian, gave up performing quite early. One day I asked how to get a vibrato like Heifetz or Kreisler. My teacher replied that, as they were geniuses, they did it in their way. *Did much of your inspiration come from other sources?* Yes, from the violinists I heard at concerts and on records. *So, from an early age you were listening to the greatest?* I was lucky to be able to do that.

When did you first start learning Paganini caprices? Not until I was sixteen and at the Academy. If I had stayed with Norbert Wethmar, I probably would have started them much sooner. *Did you have, in those days, any virtuoso aspirations?* None whatsoever. I was rather intimidated by Heifetz's recording of the **Scherzo**

Tarantelle, and realised that sheer virtuosity was not my natural direction. I now realise that my playing of one or two virtuoso pieces showed a lot of talent, but I didn't have any real idea of how to work at technique. When confronted with a passage that I couldn't play, I didn't know how to analyse or work it out. I had some problems with string crossing when playing really fast. These were not sorted out until I was in my twenties. A lot of things I did by sheer willpower, rather than by technical accomplishment.

When you went to hear one of the top soloists, how much did you feel that you would like to be in their place? I only had that feeling when hearing the concertos of Mozart, Beethoven or Brahms. Virtuoso music seemed interesting but like going to a circus. *So, temperamentally, you were always more drawn to the serious side of the musical spectrum?* Yes.

One day, I heard my teacher discussing Carl Flesch's book on violin technique with his colleague, Spencer Dyke. They were talking about Flesch's idea that, when you land on a note after a jump, the intonation can be quickly adjusted if it is very slightly out. Robjohns said he was taught to measure the distance, land on the note and stay there. Sometimes I used to hear a player landing on a note that was slightly out and being stuck with it. Some years ago, a translation was published of Baillot's 1835 book on technique. He wrote that if you land on a note that is slightly out, be prepared to adjust it, provided that you are the first to hear it. Correction is vital—you've got to learn to swindle the public in things like this.

In 1936 I played for the first time on a really good violin. A lady amateur pupil of Robjohns, who lived in Park Lane, had just bought a Stradivari and was no longer using her Francesco Ruggieri. She offered to lend it to a promising student, and I was the beneficiary. I remember how beautiful it was, but at first I didn't like its tone, being used to a powerful French instrument. However, my teacher insisted on my continuing to play it until I got used to it. About a dozen years later, in 1949, the lady contacted me to ask if I would like to buy it. She took it to W.E.Hill & Sons to find out the current valuation, but unfortunately she had lost the certificate given by them in 1932 at the time of purchase. They told her that it was not a Francesco Ruggieri, but an Italian violin, without its original scroll, worth £200. Since she had originally bought it from them for £350 she was not too pleased. I was offered it for £200, on condition that I would never sell it to them! Later that year I received a Christmas card from her, enclosing the certificate which had turned up amongst

Aged seventeen, a student at the Royal Academy of Music

some papers. It said that the scroll was not original, but that the replacement was by Andrea Guarneri, who was a maker of equal distinction. After the holidays, armed with this paper, I took the violin into Hills to update the insurance. They valued it at £850.

Were there any other events at the Academy that you recall? One lunchtime I went with a friend to Regent's Park, just behind the Academy. We took out a boat and were messing about so much that we succeeded in overturning it. I started swimming towards the bank before finding that the water was shallow enough to walk in. My blue suit was soaked through and, on top of this, there were just forty-five minutes until the orchestral rehearsal with Sir Henry Wood. Fortunately, the caretaker took us down to the boiler room to dry out. My cigarettes were ruined, the lighter no longer worked, and a current collection of cigarette cards of famous cricketers was all stuck together. Strangely, none of my fellow students noticed anything. Rather surprisingly, my mother was most amused when I got home and told her what had happened.

There was an inspiring energy in Wood's rehearsals. He always wanted good articulation and used to call out 'Rhythm in the fingers!' He made the dynamics very clear by his gestures. His style was not flamboyant, but he varied the size of the beat, pulling in his hands sharply to his body when there was a sudden piano. Before a concert, he would make the whole orchestra file by while he cranked the handle of a small harmonium to give us an A, personally checking our tuning. One day, while rehearsing a new piece by Gershwin, he asked the trumpet player if he had the new wah-wah mute to use for his solo. Receiving a negative answer, he took one out of his bag and gave it to him. The second rehearsal each week was taken by Wood's assistant, B.Walton O'Donnell, a military man, later head of the RAF band, who used to tell everyone to sit up and not to cross their legs. These sessions were rather tedious and pedestrian.

I remember being impressed by a recital of Isolde Menges, who was probably in her thirties. Richard Strauss came in 1938 to conduct his tone poem **Death and Transfiguration**, which Wood had rehearsed for a whole term. Strauss had a tremendous sense of authority. His beat was very small—in contrast to Beecham, Wood and Sargent—rather like that of Felix Weingartner, whom I played under in the London Philharmonic Orchestra.

How long were you at the Academy? I finished the four years in 1937, but then continued as a half-student. That meant that I went just for my violin lesson, which was sometimes in Mr. Robjohns' house in South Kensington. I also attended chamber music classes with the cellist, Herbert Withers. Even today at the Academy there are students who have finished their course, but stay on for a couple of years learning chamber music.

Herbert Withers played in a string quartet with his brother. One day they were rehearsing the Schubert String Quintet with Pablo Casals, guest artist on that occasion. In the interval, Withers said to Casals that it was a great honour to have him join them for the quintet. Casals answered—'Quintet?—with that tapping of your foot it was more like a sextet!'

I have memories from the late 1940s of my father making visits to Sidney Robjohns' house. He was described to me as a musician who was rather lonely, having fallen on hard times. I would be left sitting in the car all alone for about forty minutes. At the age of four or five it seemed half a lifetime. He couldn't have been a poor man if he lived in the Boltons, so in what way were they hard times for him? Having had a totally incapacitating stroke, he was completely dependent on his wife, although he could still talk with difficulty. It was a great tragedy for him, because he was a passionate Christian Scientist. This view of life seeks to put mind over matter, so it must have been very difficult for him to be debilitated physically. *Did that mean that he refused medical attention?* I don't think that he was in a position to refuse it.

* * * * *

A marvellous new work from this period was Rachmaninov's big piano solo, his **Rhapsody on a Theme of Paganini**. We were also very enthusiastic about Ravel's **Bolero** and his **Tzigane**, which I immensely enjoyed learning. I had a few lessons on it from Jelly d'Aranyi, its dedicatee. She wanted more zip and an intense vibrato. I felt a little perplexed, because her own vibrato was really rather wobbly. There was a lot of fire in her playing, but it wouldn't be considered accurate enough by today's standards. She and her sister, Adila Fachiri, were friends of my teacher. They were both nieces of Joseph Joachim.

6

Chamber Music

From the age of twelve I played a lot of chamber music. Each weekend I went with some colleagues to the house of a piano teacher friend, who lived around the corner. There I learned, over a year or two, the Mozart, Beethoven and Brahms piano quartets and all the great piano quintets.

When I started at the Academy I began by playing second violin in a string quartet. In my latter days there I formed a serious quartet and was very happy with it. *Who were the other members?* The second violinist, Jørgen Laulund, was Danish and had come to England a few months previously. He told me that his first sight of London was in a dense fog, the type then known as a pea-souper. Laulund had a fine technique and a beautiful tone—I felt lucky that he was willing to play with me. He also studied with Robjohns; somehow he had been impressed at our first encounter when, coming in for his lesson, he heard me playing the Tchaikovsky Concerto. Kenneth Essex was the violist, an all-round and tremendously enthusiastic musical talent with a very fine sound. The cellist, Terence Weil, born in Switzerland, was an exceptional musician and easy to play with. He had a wonderful sense of phrasing and impeccable rhythm. We played at the Academy and in various other places: a date at the Wigmore Hall was planned for the autumn of 1939.

What quartet concerts do you remember hearing in this period? The Budapest Quartet, at the Wigmore Hall in 1937, made a very great impression on me. The leader, Josef Roisman, came from Odessa, where he had lived in the same block of flats as Nathan Milstein. The brothers Alexander and Mischa Schneider played second violin and cello; Boris Kroyt was the viola player. I particularly remember their wonderful playing of the **Italian Serenade** of Wolf and Mozart's **Dissonance** Quartet. It was this concert that gave me the feeling that I wanted to lead a professional string quartet. *So you had a more distinct reaction to chamber music than to concertos played by top soloists?* Yes, quartets meant more to me. Apropos of that, I didn't meet any top soloists until the mid 1960s. *So you were not an autograph hunter?* No, I never liked to disturb people after a concert if I didn't know them. In the 1960s, Rudolph Serkin came to London and played with the English Chamber Orchestra at the City of London and Edinburgh festivals. The conductor was Alexander Schneider, second violin of the Budapest Quartet. When I told him that I had heard his quartet at the Wigmore Hall he said that he remembered how little they were paid for it!

How did the Budapest Quartet get its name? Originally it did come from Budapest. The initial group was led by Emil Hauser who later, after his health declined, went to Israel and became a piano dealer. *I remember meeting him at the Prades Festival.* When I heard the quartet they were on their only pre-war European tour. By then, the personnel were no longer Hungarians—they were all Russians. A story goes that, after a post-war concert in Budapest, people came round to speak to them. The Hungarians asked if they could understand what they were saying. The second violin, Schneider, replied 'We're just four Russian Jews like everybody else coming from the USA!' In those days most immigrants were Jewish.

Having heard the Budapest, I tried to find their recordings. Also I looked for records of the Kolisch and the Lener Quartets. The Lener was perhaps the most famous quartet of all in those days, with a tone quality and singing Viennese style that had something in common with that of the Amadeus Quartet. The leaders of both these groups had fairly wide vibratos.

Another quartet, which I'd never heard in concert but had admired on record, was the Busch Quartet. I remember how, after hearing the Budapest, I had to work really hard to accept the tonal world of the Busch Quartet. *How was it different?* It was like the difference between Kreisler and Huberman. Adolf Busch was a towering musician—very intense and serious, but not a person with an instantly pleasing left hand sound—it wasn't commercial. You can still get CDs of his quartet in recordings from the 1930s and '40s, and they are mighty performances. Busch was wonderful with his chamber orchestra. I used to have all his **Brandenburg Concertos**. The first time I played the fourth Brandenburg I had never heard anybody play it live, but only knew Busch's recording. I used his tempi, and it was pointed out to me by baroque specialists that one or two of the movements were outrageously fast.

7

. . . .

First Work

Did you do any part-time work while at the Royal Academy? I was already doing odd jobs for which I was paid. *Was there any pressure from your family to earn money?* No, I was just lucky, because one of my teacher's private pupils, Roberto Ferraro, was second violin for the Savoy Hotel's lunch and dinner music, and I used to deputise for him. The directors of music at the Savoy were Arthur and Jack Salisbury, two major light music violinists. We were told to play subito fortes or accents rather lightly, so as not to disturb the diners—blandness was the order of the day. We played a number of arrangements, by a Frenchman called Tavan, of popular orchestral classics. All the parts were cued so that these arrangements could be played with the instruments available. We did selections from **Tosca** and **La Bohème** with string quintet, piano, flute and clarinet. Putting in the woodwind parts on the violin was a useful experience.

In the 1930s musicians were much less ambitious. A career as a soloist or in chamber music was almost unthinkable: Albert Sammons was the only Englishman so employed. Musicians were concerned with earning their living by getting a job in an orchestra. There were just three symphony orchestras in London and no chamber orchestras. However, if you were successful in music in the 1930s you were doing very well. The national average wage was then about £150 a year. The first job I ever had was in 1937, with the Scottish Orchestra. It was not even a full week's work, about five days, and I was paid £5 15s, which was virtually double the average wage. I was just eighteen and it was the first time that I had been away from home. On arrival in Glasgow, for the first rehearsal at St Andrew's Hall (now burnt down), we were not allowed in because there was a Musicians Union meeting going on. After about half an hour someone came out and said 'We have something to celebrate—pay has been raised from £5 10s a week to £5 15s'. For hotel rooms we were to get two shillings a night instead of one and sixpence.

The Scottish Orchestra, in those days, had only a three month season in the winter. My teacher sent pupils to prepare them for a full time job. The conductor, Georg Szell, also director of the Czech Philharmonic Orchestra, seemed to me a really fine musician. He had taken over from the young John Barbirolli, who had left to conduct the New York Philharmonic. Szell was a dynamic musician who used to jump off the rostrum during rehearsals to demonstrate phrases on the piano. He was quite dictatorial, insisting on the horn section buying and learning to play German horns, rather than the older French ones. Once he said to the cymbal player, 'Terrible—it sounds like kicking the night-pot!'

I read an irate letter in the Glasgow Herald about there being too many foreigners (meaning English) in the orchestra. The writer was used to the conductor being foreign, but was unhappy that the previous leader was now demoted to make way for a young Pole, Henri Temianka, an exceptionally fine player who also played sonata recitals with Szell. There was a rumour that Temianka was paid even more than David McCallum, the leader of the London Philharmonic Orchestra.

Was there much difference in the working atmosphere before and after the war? I suppose a symphony orchestra is like being in a big club in that you're mixing with a lot of people. I remember, before the war, playing as an extra with Malcolm Sargent in the LPO. I told one of the fiddle players that I thought it was thrilling. He asked my age, which was eighteen, and retorted that I wouldn't be thinking like that in another five years. *Were many of the orchestral players in those days not enjoying music all that much?* A lot of players had technical gifts but were not particularly enamoured of music. My love of great music has not changed over the years.

Would you care to speak about the accident you had at this time, concerning your little finger? It happened on a tour with the Scottish Orchestra. We were returning to Glasgow after a concert in Aberdeen, the last of the season. I boarded the train about fifteen minutes before it left, and went down the corridor to speak to someone in one of the other compartments. I opened the door at the end of the carriage, but it wasn't a corridor train and I fell straight down on to the line. With only a narrow gap between this carriage and another train, my hand slid down it as I fell, hurting my little finger very badly. There was a greenstick fracture, so I was told to leave the bandage on for a bit. When I eventually took it off, I found that the joint had set into a rather peculiar shape. *Did you consult a specialist?* No.

Travelling to a concert

How did this affect your playing? When I put my fourth finger down, it would collapse inwards. If I was on the A string, I could easily foul the E string with it, so it was not easy to play certain chords. *Was this a major inconvenience?* It would have been if I had been learning scales in thirds, or unaccompanied Bach. There were some problems, but I found alternative fingerings. For example: to play a third in the first position, with 4th finger E on the A string, it was difficult to play a 2nd finger G on the E string—so I used a 1st finger instead, with a more arched hand. I used that sort of fingering all my life; the music I played seldom included thirds. Later, I found an early Haydn quartet slow movement, the only one that has thirds, which I found rather difficult to play well. *What year did the accident happen?* 1937. *If you'd been contemplating a virtuoso career, that would have been a major handicap.* Yes, but I was already more interested in chamber music.

How much professional work did you do in the years up to the Second World War? When I came back from Scotland in January 1938 I was depping at the Savoy Hotel and for the LPO. *Was work hard to find?* I don't know, because I wasn't actively seeking employment—rather studying most of the time. I did odd jobs, about one a week, and then went back to Scotland for another season, later in 1938.

There was a position for a number seven first violin going in the LPO. I auditioned for this, playing for Thomas Beecham and the string adviser, Lionel Tertis. I was offered the job, but my teacher told me very firmly that I would be stupid to take it. He said that I would do very well playing string quartets, which could be combined with freelance work. If I could earn money playing chamber music, I would be much better off than if I spent my time in a symphony orchestra. *So string quartets were already more interesting to you than symphonic work?* More than being an extra, at the back of the first fiddles of an orchestra.

I found it really difficult to enjoy the music for the Wagner Operas in Covent Garden, being right at the back and mixed up with the percussion and various anvils and bells; but otherwise it was very exciting doing that sort of thing. I'm very proud that I did the Ring Cycle with Weingartner at Covent Garden. The other works in the season were **Don Giovanni** and the **Bartered Bride**, which Beecham conducted. I have very distinct memories of Beecham in these works. He was rather similar to Wood, in that they both had tremendous vitality and rhythm. Beecham was very fond of Mendelssohn's **Midsummer Night's Dream Overture** which starts off with woodwind chords. He would just give an indication and the wind would come in a bit later, exactly together. *Was he a little vague in his beat?* In the way that some great conductors can be vague. A conductor who tries to beat exactly all the time can get rather stiff performances.

When you auditioned for Beecham, how did he strike you as a personality? He was a perfectly charming gentleman with a white beard; very particular about his players. When I first played in the orchestra they'd just done a tour around England, performing Sibelius symphonies. They were using larger forces for the concerts in London, and he took the trouble to rehearse those of us who hadn't played the works as a little string orchestra. At one of his Sunday Concerts we accompanied Ida Haendel at her first appearance in London. She played Mozart's Concerto in G with astonishing musical maturity and complete technical ease.

At the Courtauld-Sargent Concerts I worked with Fritz Kreisler, who played the Mendelssohn and Tchaikovsky concertos. For the Tchaikovsky, Kreisler supplied a manuscript ending for the slow movement—wanting to take a break and tune his violin before the

Finale. Also, in this series, Emanuel Feuermann played the Dvorak Cello Concerto. It was quite wonderful playing—his enormous technique and almost arrogant security was the equivalent of Heifetz. It was a great experience to hear cello playing like that in the 1930s.

Were you quite active in freelance work, once you had started with the London Philharmonic? For a few months, with the opera and concerts, it really was a busy period—then suddenly, in the middle of September 1939, it all came to an end.

8

The Advent of War

How did it feel to have a world war looming, just as your career was beginning to get going? As a twenty-year-old I knew that I would be in the army very soon after the start of any war, so I just let life happen to me and didn't resist. When talking with a group of friends I was surprised to hear a couple of them say that they would become conscientious objectors, because they couldn't possibly do anything military. A few were quite enthusiastic about volunteering for the Air Force, thinking it would be marvellous to learn to fly an aeroplane, but three of them were killed in training; a cellist, an organist and a pianist.

Train loads of children began coming out of Germany, Austria and Czechoslovakia in the few months before the war. Those we knew were all Jewish—they were the ones in danger. I have friends who came over as tiny tots in those days; one of them, Ursula Hess, plays quartets with my wife. Thousands of Jewish children were saved by an English diplomat in Prague, who arranged for their transport to England. This man is now about ninety and was knighted only recently for his work. The story is told in the recent book, **The Hitler Émigrés**, by Daniel Snoaman.

Were you ever affected in any way by anti-Semitism? Only slightly. In my area there were some young thugs who were influenced by Moseley's fascist ideas. If they looked at you and decided you were a Jew, they could become aggressive. *Did this ever happen to you?* No, because next door there was a very large Alsatian, friendly to me, which I always borrowed when I went out. *Did you borrow the dog with that in mind?* Absolutely. *Did this start around 1934?* Yes, and it continued right through the pre-war years. It seemed that the world situation was darkening, with the start of the Spanish Civil War and the entry of the Nazis into the Rhineland. I remember Neville Chamberlain's 'Peace in our time' speech, after the Germans annexed part of Czechoslovakia; heads continued to be buried in the sand in the following year, when Hitler entered Prague.

Since it wasn't that long after the First World War, there must have been a certain reluctance to go to war again? I remember people saying that the First War had been sheer carnage, with a large number of casualties. Just twenty years later it was all starting again.

When war was imminent we were told that we were liable to be called up for service: however, all university, technical college and music academy students could have a year's postponement if they wished, to complete their studies. I was twenty in May 1939, had finished my studies and didn't wish to go back. If I had taken an extra year at the Academy, I would then have been able to join an excellent orchestra at the RAF. About five or six months after the outbreak of war, the Air Force Command said that they wanted to expand their orchestra. Any students just leaving music college could apply. Violinists Frederick Grinke, David Martin, Harry Blech and Tom Carter joined, also Dennis Matthews, the pianist. I could have been in that orchestra, playing with first-class musicians and staying in the London area.

Moving up to the declaration of war, what were your activities? At the start of war in September, suddenly there were no orchestras working, no opera—nothing whatsoever happened. *Why did they stop?* Perhaps because there was the expectation that London would be bombed. I remember that Hills sent a lot of instruments out of London into storage. They also sold a few quite cheaply—it was then that William Pleeth bought his Strad cello.

The war started in September. Because of the general musical inactivity, I took the opportunity to join my parents for a holiday in Bournemouth. However I felt rather lost, because I was supposed to be in London, rehearsing for our first quartet concert at the Wigmore Hall. I had my violin with me and I was practising my parts, going for walks and just wondering what life was going to bring. *Were you resigned to going to the front and doing your bit?* I was, yes. When I originally registered, the form asked for preferences so I put down Royal Artillery. Having been good at maths, I thought that it would be interesting to work out gun trajectories.

It is natural that, at the start of hostilities, a War Office tends to function as it did in the previous war. At my medical, it was announced that I had flat feet. Officially it meant that I couldn't march very far in army boots, but later I found that I could, quite easily. Not having perfect eyesight made me A2, instead of A1. Anyone rated A2 was automatically in the Medical Corps. Spectacles with flat sides, that would go underneath a gas mask, were issued in the first few months of the war.

I was called up to the Medical Corps for training at the beginning of October. I remember saying goodbye to my parents and various friends and going by train to Bridgend in Wales, joining the 159th Welsh Field Ambulance Unit. There, with about twenty-five other boys of my age, I was taught how to put on various bandages and to handle a stretcher. Several of these chaps had just come out of jail: at the beginning of the war, anyone with less than a year to serve could volunteer. Some of them were petty London criminals. *Were they fairly rough types?* They were, but very genial.

However, I was only a month in Wales learning to be a soldier, and transferred before we had our first leave. This was rather disappointing, because a couple of these fellows were going to show me how to make some money. One had been in jail for shoplifting—the other had been caught cheating in dog racing. He told me that I could make money betting on the dogs if I would follow his advice. When putting a dog into the trap for the race, a nip on its testicles would slow it down just enough to influence the result. Somewhere, I've got a few photos with these chaps.

We used to get up at six for Reveille; it was October, and still dark. We went down from the camp to the pebble beach to do some PE. Although I was a bit vague, I was intelligent enough to realise that, in the dark, no one would notice if I slipped behind a rock. I sat down for half an hour until they had finished, then rejoined them, helping to make breakfast. Tea for a hundred and fifty men used two quarter pound packets in an old army sock. This was used as a giant tea bag in a fire bucket of boiling water. We drank out of tin bowls that held about half a pint. On the first morning I asked somebody if there was any hot water for shaving; I was told to leave myself a little tea for that.

The only increase in rank that I received was to Nursing Orderly Class Three, which showed comprehension of a very limited repertoire of bandaging and splints; it meant an extra sixpence a day and was a higher rank than private. Soon I was to get a further sixpence raise for being a bandsman.

9

. . . .

The Army Band

The Royal Army Medical Corps was stationed in Fleet, about four miles from Aldershot. Its initials, RAMC, were said to stand for **Rob All My Comrades**, from the prevailing tendency to empty the pockets of stretcher patients. They had a band and my application to join it was accepted, largely because the bandmaster was impressed by my having played with the London Philharmonic Orchestra. Within a very short time I took a dislike to the young officers, who were very arrogant and pushy; they wanted to be saluted all the time. At the beginning of the war, any recently qualified doctor was automatically registered as a lieutenant.

In my first month there I played a couple of fiddle solos at a concert; afterwards a young woman came backstage to see me. She asked if I would like to play some duets back at her place. She was a student at Trinity College, only recently wed, and living there in the married quarters. We were playing a Spohr duo when her husband came in, one of the young lieutenants. He said to her 'You just can't socialise with a private'. She told me that she was sorry, but her husband wouldn't let her play with me again.

Our bandmaster, Harry Johnson, had been a virtuoso trombone player and welterweight boxing champion of his regiment. His enthusiasm, before beginning a piece, would often make him smack his fist into his other hand, saying 'When I give you a straight left—we're off!' He was convinced that he was a great musician. The foundation for this supposed greatness lay in his own individual philosophy about rhythm. Not for him the monotony of a steady beat—his musical vision showed a more aesthetic approach. He stated proudly 'With me, no two beats are ever alike!' The sad fact is that this was true—he was constantly hurrying some beats and lingering on others, with his own incomprehensible sense of logic. Sometimes he would hold up a beat, just to catch us out. Unable to cope with the strain of this, several of the players volunteered for active service, one even going to Burma! I developed, as a survival tactic, a rather laid back attitude. Yet even I was tempted one day by an advert for trainees in arial photography, a subject I found rather interesting. However, our bandmaster would not countenance the idea of my leaving, so I was in for the duration.

I was put in the first violins. The leader of the orchestra was a regular, with the rank of sergeant, who could just about play the violin. *Where were you seated?* It wasn't at that time a full orchestra—we only had one oboe and clarinet etc. We sat three to a desk—I was number three. Number two was principal second of the BBC Welsh Orchestra and older than me. I was the youngster, but was given the solos to play. *So the two of you were able to cover up for the leader, to let him bluff his way through?* Yes.

Our principal viola had volunteered a few months before the war. He decided he preferred to play rather than to carry on with his course of taxidermy; consequently he'd been there a couple of months before any of us. One morning, he told us that he had just completed his first year. We all thought it was a long time. *You didn't have any notion of how long the war was going to last?* We had no idea.

One evening I played the first movement of the Beethoven Concerto, with the Joachim cadenza, in the Aldershot Garrison Theatre. Next morning, I was summoned to the CO's office. Perhaps I was naively expecting a compliment; instead I was told: 'Bandsman Hurwitz, last night I was sitting in the front row of the concert and I saw a grease spot on your right trouser leg. Never let that happen again. I have informed your bandmaster, so from now on all of you had better be immaculate!' After six months we abandoned khaki and were given ceremonial uniforms: blue tail suits with maroon lapels and trouser stripes—we looked rather like wine waiters. However, these colours were probably better for hiding grease spots!

The band had a collection of instruments, including eight violins, two violas and two cellos. The violins, purchased from Boosey and Hawkes, were mostly by Fagnola and Pedrazzini, two of the most successful makers of the twentieth century. When I joined the band they were five or six years old. As with the brass instruments, they were considered to have a life of twenty years, and their value was marked down a little each year from the original cost of about £30. Army violins tended to have scratches on the back from contact with the various buttons and buckles of the military uniform. One day, on returning from leave with my tin hat and haversack, I realised that I

Part of the Army Band

had left my violin on the bus. I immediately phoned the station and it transpired that someone had seen a soldier walk off with it. On reporting the loss to the company office I was asked its age. I said that it was made in 1680 and was told that it had no value. When I informed them that it was a Francesco Ruggieri, worth £350, the instrument was recovered in a few hours.

What were living conditions like during the war years, as regards food etc.? We had the normal army rations. I used to enjoy concert excursions because, late at night, when we came back in a lorry or coach, we were allowed to go to the cook house to have a large dinner of the next morning's breakfast. It was a luxury to have lots of eggs, bacon and mugs of cocoa at night and then again in the morning. In the correct army way they started cooking eggs and bacon at midnight, in a slow oven. They were like leather when served at breakfast. *Were the army rations the same as civilian rations?* Army rations were more rudimentary. Tea or coffee could be bought at break time in the NAAFI, or you could have free cocoa. If you were only earning about 75p a week and were a smoker, you would choose the free cocoa. Newspapers were on sale in the camp so I bought the Daily Telegraph each morning, partly to do the big crossword puzzle. Nowadays I can no longer do it, because my brain just doesn't work the same way any more. In those days it took me about half an hour, although I didn't always finish it.

Was there much difference between the officers' food and that of the men? We didn't know, because we didn't eat in the same places. Later, when we went abroad to Iraq and Iran, we met soldiers in the American army. We were amazed to find that the American officers ate in the same place and at the same time as the men. This seemed a more sensible arrangement. We were very jealous of them, because they had lots of tinned chicken and pineapple, flown in from the USA. The people jealous of us were the Russians—they were mostly peasants and were on pretty scanty black bread rations.

Was there anything to enjoy in the music making? Yes, we had three or four really first class jazz musicians. One of these, violinist Oscar Grasso, played in Victor Sylvester's Ballroom Orchestra. He also played the tenor saxophone so, in the band, he played the tenor sax solos and I did the violin solos. *How big was the band?* Eventually thirty-five to forty. *What were the main duties?* Going on parade once a week in the square and playing marches, also giving a concert each week at the Aldershot Garrison Theatre and other theatres in the area.

One day I was asked by the Theatre if I would appear in a variety production, dressed up as a gypsy, to play a solo with the small orchestra. I suggested **Caprice Viennois** of Kreisler. When I asked bandmaster Johnson for a week's leave to do this, he said 'Bandsman Hurwitz, I am giving you permission, and they'll be paying you ten shillings (50p) a night for four minutes work. I think you are going to do well in civilian life, but I would like you to remember that you'll never earn easier money than this!'

The army band was normally paid £40 for a concert. This money was divided three ways. One third for the band fund, one third for the conductor, and the rest was divided amongst the thirty players. I generally got three and sixpence or, if I played a solo, four shillings (20p). These sums were very attractive extras to the basic pay. Our bandmaster was a tremendous enthusiast, who wanted to play all the time. We were extremely busy, doing about three or four concerts a week in England and then in Northern Ireland. These trips were connected with recruitment. I remember, on tour, arriving at barracks where the beds were just three planks. We were issued with palliasses—canvas duvet covers, to be filled with straw from the shed next door. Someone said that the straw was damp, so I had to choose between hardness and dampness. I chose to use the straw and woke up in the night in a cloud of steam, yet managed to fall asleep again. Often we had to sleep on the floor, but there were usually plenty of blankets to rest on. I became quite a connoisseur of sleeping surfaces: wood was much more comfortable than concrete.

One day in 1941, while on tour with the band, I was looking around Canterbury Cathedral on a free morning. The verger, surprised to see someone in uniform in the cathedral, invited me to sign the visitors book. I wrote Bandsman E. Hurwitz RAMC. He looked at my name and said it was unusual. I told him that it is Russian. It so happened that, the day before, Hitler had invaded the Soviet Union. Churchill had immediately declared his support for Stalin, saying 'I would mate with the devil to defeat Hitler'. The verger said despairingly, 'Oh dear, oh dear, we're on their side now!'

Early in 1942 the head of the RAMC, Colonel Wallace Benson, came to visit us in Fleet. After listening to one of our concerts, he suggested to our bandmaster that the cellist, Dennis Nesbitt, and I could join him occasionally for a trio concert at the London headquarters in Millbank Hospital. A fiery man with a large moustache, Colonel Benson was quite a good pianist. He was proud of having, on his previous posting in the Himalayas, always managed to have his upright piano carried over the mountains with him. The concerts at the hospital were always well attended, in part with his officers, who used to relish seeing this firebrand a bit nervous.

10

The Middle East

In 1943 we went to the Middle East, first to Egypt on a troop ship, but steaming for two days out into the Atlantic to give the impression that we were going to America. We were one of the first convoys going through to Alexandria, and the Germans didn't want us to get into the Mediterranean. During the passage, in the middle of a concert for the troops on board, we were quite heavily dive-bombed. Our escort ships started releasing depth charges against enemy submarines. The bandmaster stopped and said we could go below. The nearest ship in our convoy was sunk.

On the boat I discovered an ideal place for a nap after lunch. It was the mattress store room, and these were piled up nearly as high as the low ceiling. I found that by getting on top and rolling towards the wall, I could be both comfortable and invisible. Then I discovered that the ammunition store was on the other side of the bulkhead. This time I had to choose between safety and comfort—I took a chance and chose comfort.

Army personnel in Cairo

Street scene in Cairo

Was the idea of going to the Middle East to play to the troops? The army bands played in any place that had recently been conquered by the British. *What sort of reception did you get?* The audiences were mainly British troops—we didn't get many Iranians coming to listen. We played concerts in Alexandria and at our base in Cairo. Altogether we spent a year touring round Persia, Iraq, Syria

Heavily laden army truck

The journey to Iran

and Palestine. In Iraq, the American forces had PX stores for their own forces, and we were given special permission to visit them after concerts. I bought some cigarette lighters and sold two or three to Iraqi officers. I purchased beautiful lengths of silk in the markets of Baghdad and Damascus as presents for my mother and sister and, in Iran, little paintings on ivory, which I swapped for leather handbags and wallets in Egypt.

A friendly young man, Moustafa, who spoke quite good English, ran a leather shop in Cairo. He was twenty-one and already doing quite well in business. One day, he said he was closing for a week for his wedding ceremony and honeymoon. I asked him about the girl and he said 'I don't know—I haven't seen her yet'. Later I asked if he was happy and he said, 'Well, for me she is fat enough, but a little short. I like her but, after a while, I will buy a second wife'. I enquired whether his wife would be helping him in the shop and he looked shocked at the idea. He said 'No, a wife must stay at home, because if she went out she might meet another man, or go to the cinema. My wife will be very happy at home, because she has the radio and plenty of lemonade.'

When we were in a town we were usually billeted at the YMCA. To have a camp bed there was a luxury after being in a tent on the desert sand. I also remember sleeping in a military hospital ward with twenty beds on each side; it was made of metal hoops covered with canvas. All the domestic work, washing, cooking and cleaning was done by the Indian army. This was after the war had finished in the western desert.

When we visited Baghdad under the auspices of CEMA, Council for the Encouragement of Music and the Arts, there was one designated restaurant. The menu was always the full English breakfast, three times a day. You could eat as much as you liked, so by the end of the week everyone had indigestion. Each morning the Iraqi cook woke us with the cry 'Eggy-piggy!'

It was thrilling to see the Greco-Roman ruins in the Lebanese town of Baalbek, later to be the site of a big festival. I climbed up one of the pillars and was photographed squatting at the top. The whole Middle East journey was a tremendous adventure.

All through this trip we had to lug around the band's upright piano, and the weight was increased by its wooden carrying case. We all hated having to drag it about everywhere in the desert, constantly pulling and pushing it on and off trucks. On our return to Greenock, I volunteered to stay behind as part of the unloading party. We

Moustafa in his leather shop in Cairo

noticed that all the heavy objects were being unloaded by crane; down fairly quickly to about ten feet, then more cautiously lowered, till the stevedores called out 'Right!', and the object was released. While the piano was still twelve feet up, we all cried out 'Right!' and there was the satisfying sound of splintering wood and the twanging of strings. Of course, we told the bandmaster that it was the fault of the stevedores.

In the 1960s I revisited Lebanon, Iran and Israel with the ECO and the Melos Ensemble. I never imagined that I would be paid to play in those places where I had served as a bandsman in the 1940s.

11

The End of the War

Did you come you back from the Middle East before the end of the War? We returned in the middle of 1944. As most news was censored, we hadn't heard about the V1 and V2 rockets attacking London, so were quite shocked to hear their explosions. I returned to London on leave, to find that the family home had been bombed. My mother and young sister were living out in Bletchley. At first I stayed with my father, who was residing above Warren Street Underground Station, in a very posh apartment that belonged to his firm. The place was full of Dunhill pipes and Ronson lighters that had been saved from bombed premises. My father was trying to make lists of all these items.

On another visit to London I met the cellist from my quartet, Terence Weil; we found that we were stationed only about three miles apart. He was in the Service Corps in Aldershot and we happened to be on leave at the same time. He suggested that I could share accommodation with him in St. John's Wood at the house of Harold Craxton, the distinguished accompanist and teacher. As we were approaching the house, the air raid sirens sounded. By the time we got there the house was ablaze, struck by a firebomb, so we went off to one of my friends for a few nights. Soon afterwards, the Craxtons moved to Kidderpore Avenue in Hampstead, and we moved there with them. This is the house where the Craxton Studios later came in to being.

When did you first meet Kay? In 1939. Kay was an ATS girl—a territorial reserve, stationed in Fleet, as we were. She joined up to assist in the army, and found herself washing up in the Officers' Mess. *Was she able to play?* She hadn't taken her violin with her. We met at one of the band concerts at the Aldershot Garrison Theatre and I remember just saying a few words to her after the performance. She thought that I played rather well. At the time, Kay was engaged to a young captain, and my thoughts were with a girl I'd left behind in London.

I didn't see Kay again until a chance meeting in 1944. *She was married?* And unmarried, with a daughter of two. She was studying viola at the Royal Academy of Music. One day, a fellow student asked her if he could stay for a night at her flat, as a concert would make him miss the last train back to barracks. When he arrived, she saw that he was wearing the arm band of the Medical Corps and the lyre badge of the Army Band. This led her to ask if a certain violinist, whom she remembered from 1939, was still in the band. It so happened that this bandsman was my cousin, Victor Gordon, who later reintroduced us. We began to meet regularly when I was on leave; we enjoyed going to concerts, museums and restaurants. Kay used to feed the quartet after rehearsals, which was most helpful.

I will never forget VE day in London—the excitement of being in the crowd, and later the fine view of the celebrations from the roof of Kay's flat in Holborn. *The war had taken up six of your early years: had plans for your career been put on the back burner?* I realised that I hadn't really practised in this time, having played mainly gipsy and jazz solos . . . *And did you feel that performing regularly as soloist did something for your development?* It helped my sense of projection so, in that way, it was good experience. I also learned what it was like to lead an orchestra, which I did in some of the smaller concerts.

When were you demobbed? In February 1946. The older married men were released first—those in their twenties had to wait. *Why were you kept on until February 1946?* Because that's how the army worked. One member of our band virtually had a nervous breakdown when he heard about this waiting time. I was lucky, in that my bandmaster allowed me to leave the orchestra when the war finished. I spent the last eight months of my service in a group called Stars in Battledress. It was an excellent orchestra, begun by the conductor, George Melachrino, who was a wonderful pianist, conductor and arranger of light music. He organised a lot of concerts in London. Sadly, he died young. Then I played in a smaller chamber orchestra which rehearsed at the headquarters of Stars in Battledress. It was an enormous house, near Marble Arch, so we gave concerts there. I made the acquaintance of William Pleeth, Frederick Riddle, Christopher Bunting, and Samuel Bor, who later became leader of the Scottish Orchestra.

12

. . . .

Picking up the Threads

I began reading the two books by Carl Flesch in 1944, while sheltering from the buzz bombs in the basement of the new family residence in Stoke Newington. I was fascinated by these volumes, never having read anything before about how to play the violin. They are still the two most important books written since the original violin treatise of 1835—Baillot's **Art of the Violin**. Flesch's books, published in 1910 and 1920, encompass all possibilities. Many people are now reading Volume One again because it was recently republished in Boston, edited by a very fine pedagogue called Eric Rosenblith, who made a new translation. He only did the first volume—**Violin Technique**. I don't know many people who have read Volume Two, which is entitled **Artistic Realisation**.

Were these books your main instruction at the time? I used them in place of a teacher. One of the first people I met, after the war finished and I was out of the army, was a young man called Norbert Brainin. Although he was four years younger, he knew much more about playing than I did. An Austrian, he had been interned for the first years of the war. This had given him the opportunity to learn a very large repertoire—even, he said, time to mess it up by trying alternative bowings and fingerings. His compatriots, Sigmund Nissel and Peter Schidlof, were interned elsewhere. They were all pupils of Max Rostal and possessed a more detailed knowledge of technique than I did. *What did they say about the conditions of internment?* They just spoke about the boredom, but conditions weren't particularly harsh. They had come to England as schoolboy refugees. On reaching the age of eighteen, they were automatically reclassified as enemy aliens and interned. I had some friends who were taken by ship to Canada for internment—there they were treated like criminals.

How long did it take to get your playing back on track? I started serious practice, doing as much as I could, in late 1944. I came out of the army in February '46 and my first concert was in London at the Conway Hall. It was with Terence Weil and Kyla Greenbaum, who had been at the Academy with me. I remember the programme: the Busoni Second Violin Sonata, the Liszt Piano Sonata and the Ravel Trio. Kyla was the younger sister of Hyam Greenbaum, conductor of the television orchestra and husband of Sidonie Goossens, a distinguished harpist, who died recently aged one hundred and five.

When you began to practise seriously at the end of 1944, did you have the feeling that the war was going to end? Yes, and so I felt that I had to get myself in shape to earn a living. The viola player of my string quartet, Kenneth Essex, had just come out of the Marines—he had been in a band, playing saxophone and viola. My second violin, Jørgen Laulund, was back on sick leave from the war in Burma: he returned weighing only about seven stone. Terence Weil had joined up a little later because he was younger. He was in the Stars in Battledress Orchestra and so was based in London. We were thus able to start quartet rehearsals. In 1946 we gave the first performance in England of the Shostakovitch Piano Quintet with Alan Bush, my composition teacher at the RAM.

We heard that Glyndebourne was reopening. The management had asked the successful young composer, Benjamin Britten, to write an opera for small forces, because their budget was limited. He wrote the **Rape of Lucretia**, and that led to the formation of the English Opera Group. It is written for an orchestra of string quintet, wind quintet, harp and conductor who also plays piano continuo. He auditioned my quartet and we were pleased to get the job. We were due to begin rehearsals in June 1946, but discovered that our second violinist and cellist could not be demobbed until five or six weeks after the rehearsals were starting. Ben Britten asked if I could find two first-class substitutes to come in for those few weeks. I suggested a very talented cellist, Martin Lovett, who was only nineteen; also a fine young violinist, Peter Schidlof, who was later to join the Amadeus Quartet as violist. Our bass player, Eugene Cruft, had once been principal bass in Queen Victoria's orchestra; a man of seventy with an enormous moustache. He was in charge of booking a chamber orchestra, at that time nameless, for the new Third Programme of the BBC. Founder members of this group included the Amadeus and Hurwitz Quartets.

I was rather pleased, around this time, to receive a letter from Jewish Educational Aid Assistance, the organisation that had helped me to pursue my studies. They asked if I could repay some of the money they had lent me, because they were still helping people. By then £300 was for me a relatively modest sum, because I was earning £35 per week leading the chamber orchestra at Glyndebourne.

13

. . . .

The Post-War Period

The Forties was a decade of austerity, both during the war and after. Britain was virtually bankrupt after the war, so food rationing continued for many years. There were lots of shortages—many things that one couldn't buy, but it didn't matter. I remember Kay making me a dressing gown out of an army surplus blanket.

How was the spirit of the times after the war? Absolutely wonderful. After Labour's landslide victory in 1945 we had a new administration under Clement Attlee. *My parents, lifelong Conservatives, actually used their car to help the Labour Party ferry voters to the polling station. They were fed up with the Conservatives and wanted to get rid of them—later they bitterly regretted it.*

So there was a feeling of a new beginning? Yes, and there was a lot of work around. *How much was there a feeling of a more democratic society, less class-ridden than before the war?* I didn't think in terms of democracy and class. I was a musician, so it could be said that I was in what was, historically, the servant class. At the end of our first rehearsal at Glyndebourne, Mr. Christie, the owner, took Benjamin Britten, Kathleen Ferrier, Peter Pears, the other singers and the producer off to lunch. The orchestra was sent round to the kitchens for sandwiches. To me this was totally normal, because I was used to playing concerts in officers' messes.

One or two of the jazz musicians I had known in the army band helped me to get into the gramophone and film music session world. They knew that I was trying to earn some money to subsidise my rehearsals of serious music. I found myself doing a certain amount of work that paid roughly three times as much as an orchestral engagement. It was ideal for me to have five days to practise followed by two days of sessions.

After our work with Britten, our quartet soon got quite a few engagements. One day we were playing at a music club where our hosts, good Conservatives, told us that their five-year-old son had said 'My uncle's given me a whole pound; can I put it in the Post

Pablo Casals

Office and save it?' His mother had replied 'No dear, just leave it with me, because if it goes to the Post Office it will go to that wicked Mr. Attlee: let's wait until dear Mr. Churchill comes back'.

At a Prom, just after the war, I heard Pablo Casals play the Schumann Cello Concerto. I cannot think of any other instrumentalist who could find the heart of a phrase so unerringly. He had lucid powers of musical analysis, great insight and a beautiful and concentrated sound.

I was one of the extras from the start of the newly formed Philharmonia Orchestra in 1947. It was very exciting to work again with soloists such as Heifetz and Schnabel. I was impressed with the conducting of Igor Markevitch, Issy Dobrowen as well as Guido Cantelli, who died soon after in a plane crash.

I was in the orchestra when Artur Schnabel recorded all Beethoven's piano concertos with Issy Dobrowen at the Abbey Road Studios. In the first session, after playing one of the movements, we heard the playback. Schnabel said 'Well, I don't sound like that: I'm going to get a cup of coffee while you get it right!' Those were dangerous days, because sometimes Walter Legge used to alter the balance himself after an artist had agreed to everything. *In what direction did he make changes?* He occasionally decided, if there was a mistake in the accompaniment or if he wanted a woodwind solo to come out more pungently, to use a 'take' other than the one chosen by the soloist.

Someone once asked Schnabel why his recitals were so serious. He replied 'My recitals, I like to think, are like a visit to an important city. In everybody else's there is lighter music towards the end. This is like a holiday when architecture is viewed in the morning, which might be their Bach; an art gallery later in the day, which could be Beethoven or Schubert and then, after dinner, they end up in a brothel. In my recitals there's no brothel!

I went on tour with Edwin Fischer, who was playing concertos by Bach, Mozart and Beethoven. I asked him how he managed to characterise these composers, who were so different from each other. He replied, quite seriously 'When I play Beethoven, I am Beethoven; when I play Mozart, I am Mozart.' He was convinced that he was in touch with them.

My late distinguished colleague, Suzy Rosza, was married to Martin Lovett of the Amadeus Quartet. Very recently I attended her eightieth birthday party, and she reminded me of how we had shared a seat in the New London Orchestra at the Cambridge Theatre in the 1947–8 opera season. The conductor, who was outstanding, was Alberto Erede who later became principal conductor at La Scala, Milan. In the performances of **La Traviata**, when the tenor wandered off, singing to himself unaccompanied, his pitch always used to get flatter and flatter. Erede, as he brought in the final pianissimo chord, would cover his ear wincingly. This orchestra was founded by Alec Sherman, a good violinist who conducted the regular Sunday concerts at a big hall in the East End, called the People's Palace. He was about 5′ 4″ and he was sometimes helped with the administrative work by his brother, who was 5′ 3″. One day, when they were together in the hall, someone asked their mother which one was the conductor. She answered 'The tall one'.

I also joined the Boyd Neel Orchestra, initially as sub-leader. It was a first-class string group. The leader, Maurice Clare, was older than me. He was an exceptionally gifted Scottish violinist, but not an easy man, having a slightly arrogant personality. He was absent quite often doing chamber music concerts, so I had quite a few opportunities to lead. Boyd Neel was an amateur musician who was also a doctor. On one occasion, immediately after a concert, he had to go straight to the local hospital to deliver a baby. He commissioned Benjamin Britten to write a work for a festival: it was his **Variations on a Theme by Frank Bridge**. Another attraction of this orchestra was the visits by George Enescu, an unforgettable musician and a truly great man.

After three years I left the Boyd Neel and joined the Jacques Orchestra as leader. They did mostly choral concerts and I wanted to

Dressed for the occasion, with Breta Graham (l.) and Eileen McCarthy

play those marvellous violin solos in the **St. Matthew Passion**. Dr. Reginald Jacques, who conducted, was an academic. I remember, at a rehearsal, being confronted by an edition of something with a very involved written-out trill. I told the section 'Don't do it like that—that's only to be bothered about by Mus. Bacs'. Jacques looked a little hurt and said 'But I'm a Mus. Bac.!' I led the Jacques Orchestra at the first Edinburgh Festival in 1948 and performed Bach's E major Concerto.

Soon after the end of the war I began to have a very strange feeling—that I did not want to die stupidly in an accident. As a result I became a little apprehensive when crossing a road, or when I was in a rocking tube or a fast train. Only recently I realised that this was probably a reaction to the stress of everything we had lived through during the war years. This feeling, however, only lasted for a few months.

Then, in 1946, after playing at Glyndebourne, we travelled to Amsterdam with Britten, doing **The Rape of Lucretia**. There I met an old school friend, who had a good job in finance at Shell Oil. The work finished on a Saturday and the orchestra was due to fly home the next day. My friend suggested we spend the Sunday together, returning on Monday morning. I found that the price of a single air ticket was rather high, so in the end I went back with the orchestra. The next day my friend's plane crashed while landing at Heathrow, and he was killed. After that I didn't fly again for three years.

14

. . . .

Marriage

Kay's maiden name was Crome; she is probably descended from the distinguished Norwich painter, John Crome (1768–1821). When I informed my parents that we were planning to marry, my father didn't mind, but my mother wasn't exactly pleased with me for wanting to marry a non-Jewish girl with a two-year-old daughter. Her initial reaction was to take to her bed for three months! Later, however, she accepted the situation and decided to get up for the wedding.

Before tying the knot we needed to find a suitable flat. One day on a session, John Francis, the flute player, said that he was moving, so a flat in his house in St. John's Wood would be available. By a strange coincidence this was the flat where, a few years before, Kay had first tried playing a viola. She had been rehearsing with John's wife, the harpsichordist Millicent Silver. John came by and commented that Kay had a really big sound, which he thought would work well on the viola. They got one out from under the harpsichord for her to try. Soon after, she was able to purchase an old English viola from her great uncle. It is amazing how instrument prices have changed over the years—the agreed price of £20 included a fine Tubbs bow that had been bought from its maker.

Having sorted out our accommodation, we finally married in August 1948 in a registry office in Holborn. It was a rainy day and there was some problem with the underground trains—I remember one of my aunts arriving in a great hurry just as we were coming out of the ceremony. A year later we had to move, so we bought a house in West Heath Drive in Hampstead. We let out an upstairs flat and a couple of rooms, leading a rather bohemian lifestyle, with many visitors and people coming to stay—it was a very happy, harmonious household. The introduction of newfangled devices, such as a washing machine and an electric sewing machine, caused much excitement. I remember Kay making various items of clothing for daughter Jackie, then aged seven, who was about to visit Switzerland with our

With Kay, around the time of our marriage

then au pair, who came from that country. This was Elspeth Iliff, later to become a distinguished violin teacher and vice-president of the European String Teachers Association.

Since her days at the Royal Academy, Kay had done a lot of work. She played with the Hallé Orchestra under Barbirolli, the Liverpool Philharmonic, the International Orchestra and, later on, in the Goldsborough Orchestra. She joined the University of East Anglia Quartet which was theoretically based in Norwich. However, her generous nature never allowed her to be ambitious and she was always putting the family first.

Our son, Michael, was born in 1949. Kay was unwell for about six months after the birth and we were enormously helped by Anita Lasker, an early member of the Goldsborough Orchestra, who was living in our house. Anita has recently become well known for her radio talks and her book about wartime experiences in concentration camps. Michael was a very sociable baby who didn't like to be left alone in bed in the evenings, so we were obliged to bring him downstairs to join the company.

15

Goldsborough Orchestra

Our nameless group at the BBC eventually took the name Goldsborough Orchestra. Arnold Goldsborough, who was there from the beginning, was a musicologist, choral conductor and harpsichord player. The orchestra was getting more and more work on the radio, being an excellent little group. Later, in 1960, it changed its name to The English Chamber Orchestra. In his conducting, Goldsborough was working with players fairly new to baroque music. His idea of a forte chord was not a hard accent, but more a cushioned emphasis. As he gave this beat, he would pull himself backwards, looking as if he regretted the action. He liked to minimise vibrato, a style of playing that we were not used to. *Was stylistic attitude mostly conjectural amongst musicians in Goldsborough's day?* It was considered an interesting byway, but wasn't yet part of the music industry. Arnold Goldsborough liked a steady tempo, saying that there is then much more opportunity for subtle phrasing. He was rather an unusual man, because he claimed he could play Bach and Handel as if he hadn't heard anything that had been written afterwards. He thought that he could totally immerse himself in that period. However, I heard him playing Brahms, Schubert and Chopin excellently on the piano.

In this group I began, in 1947, as principal second. The first leader was Norbert Brainin, who was better known than I was, having won the Flesch prize just after the war. Unfortunately, after a few weeks, he was forbidden by the union to do this job, as he was not a member. After Norbert they had a couple of other leaders, who considered Arnold's views on ornamentation and phrasing to be just stupid—they didn't last for more than a few weeks. So, after a few months, virtually by default, I became the leader.

Goldsborough's assistant, who was also the producer, was the musicologist Basil Lam. Goldsborough was usually rather disorganised: when Lam asked him to do a run through for the purposes of timing, he would often stop in the middle to rehearse something.

Arnold Goldsborough

One day, having a programme consisting of eight pieces by the eighteenth-century composer, Samuel Scheidt, I asked him for the running order, just five minutes before the live broadcast. He said, irritability, 'It starts with the Scheidt'. I said 'Everything is by Scheidt'. He retorted 'I'm trying to get right this articulation in the trumpets—don't bother me with irrelevancies'. Sometimes, when a broadcast was going well over time, Lam would creep around the orchestra while we were playing, putting a card on each stand saying something like 'Cut No. 17'. Goldsborough had no interest in such small matters as timing.

One day in a rehearsal, when I had just played a small cadenza in a Handel work, he said 'Manny, that's no use—you sound like Kreisler'.

Gradually this small orchestra became the one that every visiting conductor wanted for broadcasts. There was quite a lot of moaning from the other chamber orchestras about us getting too much. We were probably working two or three times each week, which produced a significant chunk of our income. I learnt an enormous amount while playing in this group. What I loved was doing most of the Bach cantatas and many of the Handel operas. The orchestra was systematically going through everything it could find from the period.

16

Hurwitz Quartet

Were you enthusiastic about the development of your quartet? Yes, and it gradually got quite a few engagements. After our work with Britten we started rehearsing string quartets seriously. We were pleased and excited to be offered a considerable number of concerts at music clubs around the country. Being innocent English-trained musicians, we said yes to any reasonable request for our services. In our first season, 1947–8, we must have played about thirty-five works. I remember playing the three quartets of Brahms and his Clarinet Quintet with Frederick Thurston, a great player, who helped us prepare the work. We also played Hindemith's Quartets Nos. 3 & 5. I felt very happy if, at times, rather stressed by the number of works I had to learn. We had some excellent coaching from Laslo Lajthe. He was a friend of Kodály and Bartok and head of the Conservatory in Budapest; he had been given a year's sabbatical to write a film score for Beckett's **Murder in the Cathedral.** Lajthe was most inspiring, in spite of using such remarkable phrases as 'Very sentimary—play with a tear in the ear'. We performed his **Five Studies for String Quartet** at the Wigmore Hall.

After we had given several broadcasts for the BBC, their head of music, Herbert Murrell, offered us a contract. This would have involved various activities, including playing for religious services and being coached by someone we considered to be of the old school. We turned down the offer as we didn't want more instruction. I have always told my pupils about how differently the Amadeus Quartet worked, performing just six works in their first season. As pupils of Rostal and Flesch, they had the most un-English idea of learning works in depth and perfectly. When I was at the Academy, any student showing virtuoso tendencies was considered freakish. We didn't think so much about improving the group as doing a good professional job. I have a couple of recordings from broadcasts which do sound good. I tended to be supercritical in

Hurwitz Quartet
(Courtesy Jørgen Laulund)

rehearsals, while not being irreproachable myself—I couldn't have been very easy to work with. However we enjoyed playing together and, as a group, we had a lot of talent. In 1948, John Amis wrote a joint review of both our quartet and the Amadeus, wondering which one would last longer. Strangely, on a few occasions, a BBC announcer having successfully negotiated the names Emanuel Hurwitz and Jørgen Laulund, stumbled on Kenneth Essex, the only English name in the quartet.

The quartet provided only about twenty per cent of my income. At the Cheltenham Festival, where we gave the première of Bernard Stevens' first quartet, we were paid 8 guineas (£8.40) each out of which we had to pay our travel and hotel. The next day, while the others returned to London, I stayed on to play in Victor Sylvester's Band for the Festival Ball, earning £10 just for the evening.

Around this time, during a quartet rehearsal, a young man called Gervase de Peyer turned up and asked us to play the Brahms Clarinet Quintet with him. We played a couple of movements and I told him that he played marvellously, but that we were already performing these works with his teacher, Frederic Thurston.

Jørgen Laulund was also playing solo concerts and did some

broadcasts in the early 1950s. In 1951 he left the quartet, wanting to see if he could become a first violin. As a replacement I invited Granville Jones, who was wanting to leave another quartet where he was not allowed to play out. As a concerto player he felt more at home in our group. Granville was an innocent personality who didn't realise how good he was. He became leader of the Boyd Neel Orchestra, the Philomusica and, later, the LSO. He eventually founded his own quartet, named after his son Delmé.

However, by 1953, I was feeling that our quartet just didn't play well enough to become international. It was getting a little less work, and I didn't know what to do about it. I was very idealistic in those days so, having made the decision, I announced that I was going to leave. *How did the others feel about this?* Granville didn't mind very much—when he wasn't playing quartets, he would be off playing the Tchaikovsky Concerto. I have always remained good friends with our viola player, Kenneth Essex, who has also had a distinguished career. However, our cellist was very annoyed with me and, when he started a new group, the Melos Ensemble, he refused to ask me to lead it.

When you disbanded your string quartet, you were turning your back on a very important body of musical works. Yes, but immediately after that I started the London String Trio and Piano Quartet. Watson Forbes had been a violin pupil of Ševčík but later changed to the viola. He was a superb chamber music player and a fine musician. Vivian Joseph, the cellist, had an exceptionally fine tone; his was romantic music making of the highest class. We played in a number of concerts and broadcast the trios of Mozart, Beethoven, Schubert, Dohnányi, Webern, Schoenberg, and Berkeley. Then, wanting to expand our repertoire, we invited a wonderful pianist from Vienna, Edith Vogel, to join us in piano quartets. Edith was a great musician, much appreciated for her broadcasts and recitals of Beethoven and Schubert. She had a terrifying integrity, wanting to rehearse everything thoroughly in order to know exactly what we were doing. We gave many performances but, after some time, Edith became too busy to continue. She was replaced by James Gibb, who is still a very dear friend of mine. He is a warm romantic player with a big style. He retired only a few years ago from his position as principal piano professor at the Guildhall School of Music.

17

. . . .

Finding my Violin

My Ruggieri violin had a fine quality, but not quite enough volume for the work I was doing. In the early 1950s I was playing on an Amati, on loan from the Royal Academy. Initially, I had borrowed a J.B.Guadagnini and Jørgen Laulund had borrowed the Amati, but we had swapped, because this brought about a better balance in the quartet. I felt very attracted to the big sound of this Amati violin.

In 1952 I found the wonderful Antonio and Hieronymus Amati violin of 1603 that I played for the rest of my career. Alfred Cave, a distinguished player in his day, had been leader of the City of Birmingham Symphony Orchestra and of the Aeolian String Quartet from 1942–52. He had bought this Amati for £400 in 1937 from Hart, a shop that closed just after the war. When he decided to retire, he had it done up by Charles Langonet, who fitted a new bass bar, bridge and sound post.

I heard about this violin from Watson Forbes, who told me that it sounded even better than the Amati I had on loan. However, the new bass bar took a little while to play in. I first heard the violin when I went to hear my friend Raymond Cohen play the Brahms Concerto. He was hunting for a good instrument at the time (later on he bought a great Strad). When I went backstage to see him he said I could have the Amati, because for him it didn't have enough sizzle. It was a bit on the woolly side when I first tried it and took four or five months to settle, after which it sounded quite wonderful.

Cave wanted £1,000 for it. This was more than I could afford, having recently bought my first house. It was fortunate that a violin expert friend of mine, Albert Cooper from Winchester, was very impressed with the fiddle. He said that he would try to buy it. He sold three violins, including a Rocca, for which he received £300. He gave Alfred £950 and a gold-mounted engraved Tubbs bow, which in those days was worth about £35. He bought the Amati, and was exceptionally generous in that he never even took it home, but left it with me on loan. Three years later I told him I was saving up to buy

The 1603 Brothers Amati violin that I played for forty years
(Courtesy Albert Cooper)

the violin. He wouldn't consider selling it, but said the loan could be for an indefinite period. He thought that if I owned it, I might later sell it if trying to buy a Strad. That was why he didn't want to sell.

This is the violin that I have used since then. It has a wonderful quality and is a very robust sounding instrument. Over the years, whenever violinist colleagues were considering the purchase of a top quality violin, they would bring it round to my house to see if the tone was as strong as the Amati.

When I was approaching my eightieth birthday, I felt that there was a danger that I could fall on the fiddle and smash it. I had been the last owner of several cars and didn't want anything to happen to a virtually mint instrument of 1603. I had, by then, other violins I could play and teach on so, with Albert's permission, I passed it on to my exceptionally gifted pupil Anthony Marwood, who played on it until early 2005, when he acquired a magnificent Carlo Bergonzi.

18

. . . .

Melos Ensemble

The Fifties, at first rather slowly, saw the first real economic expansion since the Twenties. After the depression and the war it was a time of normality and conformity. The first passenger jets were introduced and television began to dominate the living room. The conflict of ideologies with the Soviet Union intensified the cold war, especially with the launch of the Sputnik.

I can recall from 1950 the announcement of the death of George Bernard Shaw, at the age of ninety-three. In the 1880s he had worked as a music critic, calling himself **Corno di Bassetto.** I had his complete works and enjoyed reading them. Another distinguished veteran, Arturo Toscanini, I heard conducting the BBC Symphony Orchestra. *Was he very charismatic?* He was a small, dynamic man who made the orchestra sound wonderful. I went to two concerts; one was a Brahms programme that began with the **Tragic Overture**. Toscanini somehow forgot that he was to perform this piece and went straight into the Second Symphony. The orchestra began the Overture, so he had to adjust quickly.

The Royal Festival Hall opened in '51, and we soon experienced its original dry acoustics. This coincided with the Festival of Britain, a joyous occasion; our children, Jackie and Michael, enjoyed the tree walks and the pleasure gardens. A few weeks later a Conservative government returned, and Churchill obliterated all traces of the Festival, the architecture of which he considered three-dimensional socialist propaganda. I remember the start of The Goon Show in '53, one of the major catalysts of social change that undermined the stuffiness of the old order. This was my sort of humour—I felt that they were successors to the Marx Brothers, whose films I have always loved. The Hungarian revolt in '56 brought many musicians over as refugees. Soon after, our unfortunate Suez venture brought petrol rationing. I gave £90 for a big Austin Sixteen, which was allowed more coupons than our Morris Eight.

* * * * *

The Melos Ensemble
(Courtesy William Waterhouse)

The Melos Ensemble was formed in 1955. Terence Weil, still annoyed with me for breaking up our quartet, asked Raymond Cohen to lead the group. Raymond only stayed for a year, because the group was getting engagements which coincided with his concerto dates. The first time I heard him had been in 1946, with John Barbirolli and the Hallé playing Bach, Mozart and Brahms concertos quite magnificently.

Then Eli Goren, another wonderful musician, became the leader, but after a year he became very busy with his Allegri String Quartet. When he too left the Melos they were forced to ask me. *Did your cellist create any opposition?* Not by then, no, he just tolerated me. Whenever he was going to criticise something, he would say 'I know I can't play the cello, but . . .' because we were always getting at him about his technique in the upper register of the instrument. As a musician however, he was excellent. *I heard him play with the Melos at South Place in 1958 and was quite mystified by the tone he made—it was like a double bass. Was it his instrument?* He played an enormous amount of continuo, and was invited by the specialists because of his rather boomy sound. He had an Amati cello, and then a Gofriller. *Do you remember the Amati as being rather indistinct?* Yes, it was a bit woolfy. I know that on radio recordings they had to take care to get enough cello sound for balance. I was often annoyed because I felt he had the microphone too much on his side, and that I didn't sound big enough.

Ivor McMahon was the second violinist, a very thoughtful musician who was totally reliable rhythmically. Cecil Aronowitz was a violist with a wonderful musical instinct; everything sounded right from the first rehearsal. He was a very relaxed player from whom I learned a lot about playing comfortably. Adrian Beers had the best intonation I have heard on the bass. He played immaculately together with Terence.

Richard Adeney played with us in the occasional work involving flute—an aristocratic player who was also principal flute with the LPO. I first met Peter Graeme, the oboist, in 1938; a musician with a fine sense of ensemble and rhythm. Gervase de Peyer was simply one of the very greatest clarinettists, with a sumptuous tone and noble phrasing. William Waterhouse, the bassoonist, was a player of exceptional intelligence; he was then also principal bassoon of the London Symphony Orchestra.

The horn player, Neill Sanders, combined musicality and virtuosity with an extraordinary accuracy. Pianist Lamar Crowson was clearly a born chamber musician, able to play with a big style and also a fine textural control. Our harpist, Osian Ellis, was unsurpassed, a great player. James Blades, the brilliant percussionist, was a welcome addition in contemporary works—he was a joy to work with.

The first time I played with this group was at one of the BBC Invitation Concerts, which took place in the Concert Hall in Portland Place. The Beethoven Septet, which has quite a virtuoso part, was on the programme. As all the other players knew the piece well I got very little rehearsal—I had to practise it by myself. Usually I had enough talent to sight-read a part, finding little to practise on my own. A number of passages in the Beethoven quartets needed some working out, as did some of the Bartoks. I remember finding the first Tippett quartet very difficult rhythmically.

We played many concerts around England and in festivals in Aldeburgh, Cheltenham and Edinburgh. For me it was very convenient when both the orchestra and the Melos were in the Edinburgh Festival at the same time.

I remember that, as soon as I had finished playing the Schubert Octet for the first time, I had to drive to Cardiff where, the next day, I was broadcasting the Bruch Concerto. I did various concerto performances, but eventually stopped doing this because I couldn't afford to take a few days off work to prepare them.

What I most remember about the Fifties was the sheer amount of work I was doing. If I went on tour for a week with the orchestra I would, on returning, go straight off on another one with the Melos. It was around this time that the management said that we needed some alternative leaders for the orchestra, because the Melos Ensemble was using most of the section leaders: the five strings, oboe, clarinet, bassoon and horn. Sometimes, when the Melos had got an engagement, the orchestra had no principals, so a number of co-principals were engaged. I was grateful to Quintin Ballardie for introducing me to Kenneth Sillito, who became co-leader, and who has since had a distinguished career leading the Gabrieli Quartet and the Academy of St. Martin in the Fields.

In 1959 the first records of the Melos were made on the L'Oiseau-Lyre label. Later the group recorded for EMI. Most of these recordings were eventually transferred from LP to CD and many of them are still available.

* * * * *

Our daughter Jackie enjoyed singing from an early age and had received some voice training. Her secondary school gave the opportunity to take part in a few operas. From the age of thirteen she studied at the Hornsey College of Art, initially in the junior department. Subsequently she specialised in jewellery at the Royal College of Art.

Michael, seven years younger than Jackie, started the cello when he was eight. Kay had some friends with musical children of the same age as Michael and she had the idea of getting them together in our house on Saturday mornings to form a small orchestra. After four weeks there were thirty young players, so we hired the hall in King Alfred's School. We called this organisation Young Music Makers. Before long the number had grown to a hundred and twenty. There were different orchestras and even one for the parents to play in.

In 1969, the name was changed to Youth Music Centre, or YMC. Today, more than two hundred children take part. Many past students have become well known players.

19

English Chamber Orchestra

The Sixties brought a revolt against the conformity of the Fifties, mainly amongst the younger generation. 1961 saw the first man in space and 1969 the first moon landing. It was a decade that brought many changes. The Cold War intensified with the building of the Berlin Wall. When it was finally pulled down in 1989, a violin maker we knew there sent us a small piece of it. I had always been fond of jazz but, in the Sixties, I gradually became horrified by the commercialisation of music. '63 was the year the Beatles became famous, but I was mystified that people thought this to be significant music. Then there was the Profumo scandal—he was the son of Baron Profumo who had given money for the Huberman Scholarship I won on entering the Academy. This was soon followed by the return of a Labour government, which I was happy about. At the time of the Six Day War in '67 I was working at Aldeburgh, and I remember that there was a lot of sympathy and concern for Israel.

In '68 there was the revolution in Prague—we had played there just a few weeks before. When it all began, many refugees were coming into England and there was an appeal on the radio for families who had spare beds. Kay rang the number given, as we had a small flat in our house that was available. We offered to pick them up and were told that there was a family of five in Finchley—which is where we live. They had been sleeping on the floor in the house of the mother of one of my pupils.

They turned out to be the family of the lady who had fed us tea and cakes at the British Embassy in Prague—quite a coincidence. Her husband was a journalist who had taken television film of the fighting. They had spent all night developing the film, then she stuffed it down her trouser leg to get it into the British Embassy. At the entrance, the Russian soldiers looked through her bag and found lots of sandwiches, put there as a diversion. As they were hungry, they took the sandwiches and let her through. At the border they got through the customs by casually reading Pravda.

How different was your life in the Sixties? I think the Sixties were for me an even more busy continuation of the Fifties. I was often on tour with both the orchestra and the Melos Ensemble. We managed to tailor the Melos tours into periods which were not quite so frantic with the orchestra. We did a couple of Melos tours to the USA, managed by the famous impresario, Sol Hurok. On the outward flight of the first tour, we encountered some unusual clear air turbulence over Greenland. It gave the plane a shock that temporarily knocked out two of the engines. It was a rough start to six weeks of travelling, during which we played the Schubert Octet nineteen times. Each night the new audience stimulated us to approach the work freshly. The sole exception was at a very expensive private school, where some of the audience members were simultaneously taking part in a photographic competition.

On the second tour my friend, Leonard Friedman, was standing in for Ivor McMahon. Friedman had never played the Brahms Clarinet Quintet with us, so he brought our recording with him and a portable player. When he tried to plug it in he succeeded in fusing all the lights of the hotel. On both tours we travelled in two large cars. There was a 55 mph speed limit, but the agency was happy to pay the odd speeding fine that we incurred.

* * * * *

Why, in 1960, did the Goldsborough Orchestra change its name to The English Chamber Orchestra? We were asked by agents if we could consider changing our name for touring Europe, because in some European countries people found it very difficult to pronounce Goldsborough. I remember discussing the change of name at Aldeburgh, with both the management and Benjamin Britten. At one point, Britten asked if we would consider calling it the Melos Orchestra. The management was absolutely appalled by this idea. *Why?* Because then the orchestra wouldn't be able to function on days the Ensemble was playing. I didn't want it to be called The English Chamber Orchestra, because I felt that with names like Aronowitz, Weil and Hurwitz, people might sneer at it being called English. *Yet you were English.* Yes, but Cecil was South African and Terence was originally Swiss. I asked if it would help if I changed my name to Carruthers. When the members of the Amadeus Quartet chose the name, many people thought it uncomfortable and difficult. We realised later that if something is good and successful the name becomes accepted. I think the biggest handful we ever had was Neville Marriner's Academy of St Martin in the Fields. We thought that was far too long. More recently, there has been the Orchestre Revolutionaire et Romantique and the Orchestra of the Age of Enlightenment. Such names have become fashionable.

What proportion of your work was abroad? Probably half—or a little less. If playing in France, Germany, Switzerland or in the low countries, we would often take our own cars. Sometimes, with the ECO, we took an 8 am plane to Paris for a 10 am rehearsal. Then, after the evening concert, we would return at 8 next morning for a rehearsal at 10 in London. We also went to Italy, Greece, Austria, Lebanon and Iran with the ECO. With the Melos, we played in many of those countries, plus Denmark, Sweden, Finland, Yugoslavia and Poland.

There were several other foreign tours, including various countries in South and Central America. At a hall in Mexico City, I remember the incredible glass curtain in front of the safety curtain. The evening after our concert, I returned to hear the Warsaw Piano Quintet. It was led by the virtuoso violinist, Bronislaw Gimpel. Afterwards he introduced me to the pianist, Spielmann who, by chance, I met shortly afterwards in London at the home of Felix Vandyl. Spielmann told me that he had survived the whole war in Warsaw. He wrote a much publicised book of this experience, which was also made into a film. Later in the 1940s he used to accompany Bronislaw Huberman. One one tour, Huberman had broken his right wrist in a plane crash. I asked Spielmann if he too had been injured. He said that since plane tickets were rather expensive he, as the accompanist, had been sent by train.

In Argentina I met a cousin whom I had not seen since I was four. He looked so much like me that, when I showed Kay photos of him, she asked where I had found that suit.

I remember working for two gramophone companies with the ECO. At the Walthamstow Town Hall for one company from 10–1, and from 2.30–5.30 in the Watford Town Hall for the other company: then, at 7.30 pm, having a live broadcast with the Melos, in the Maida Vale Studios. *How did your concentration and health handle that?* One of my Alexander friends said I was very lucky to have a strong back. Occasionally I remember getting a bit tired in the last hour of an orchestral session at night. *Did you feel any pain?* No. I didn't get any pains at all, because I always took care to be in as good physical shape as possible. For me, correct body use is of great importance. I learnt a lot about the Alexander Technique in the 1940s: people gradually discovered it in the following decades. Certain friends, who were not particularly good instrumentalists, became Alexander teachers—I've only known a handful of top-class instrumentalists who did.

Something I used to dislike was having to drive to a rehearsal for an evening concert. I have always felt sleepy for an hour or so in the early afternoon, even if I haven't eaten anything. That's just part of the way I'm built physically. When in my teens I used to enjoy a little siesta after lunch. In the army, I took a nap for twenty minutes after lunch, before an afternoon parade or rehearsal. When recording with the Melos, we would do a session from 10–1 in the morning, and then another from 6.30–9.30. With the quartet recordings for Decca in the 1970s it was 10–1 and 2.30–5.30, which was harder for me. I like to ask my students whether they can spot which movements were recorded in the afternoon.

Some years ago I was at my colleague Kenneth Essex's house. He said he had just found a tape of our broadcast of Beethoven and Dohnányi string trios. He put it on and I said 'This Beethoven's OK, but it hasn't got quite as much bounce as I like to hear in it'. He said 'Do you remember that we rehearsed it in the morning after you'd come back in a sleeper from an ECO concert in Liverpool. You crawled under the piano and went to sleep for half an hour before we recorded it.'

How often did you play as soloist with the ECO? Not frequently, perhaps half a dozen times a year, but very often I'd play in the Brandenburg Concertos. The orchestra was always small, so one couldn't go any further forward in time than a Mozart concerto or the Beethoven **Romances**. I have a lot of old programmes from this period which remind me of performances that I had totally forgotten about.

I first worked with cellist Paul Tortelier in the late 1950s with the orchestra at the Bordeaux Festival. His Haydn Concerto in D was really great playing—it had technical mastery, was expressive and always in good taste. He was a man of great intensity and enthusiasm. Some years later, just before going onstage to conduct a Haydn symphony in London, he grasped the lapels of the first horn, who had a particularly difficult part, predicting confidently 'You will not be nervous tonight!'

Are there any other particular memories from this period? I remember many tours and Festivals in the early 1960s, and concerts with Charles Mackerras, who used to perform slightly unusual works. We did a concert in collaboration with Rudolf Baumgartner and his orchestra, the Lucerne Festival Strings. With two orchestras on the stage there were about forty of us in total.

Slava Rostropovitch performed several times with us. He played Vivaldi and Haydn concertos and, later on, the Britten Symphony. He has transcendental technical gifts—a complete musician and a tremendous personality. Sometimes in rehearsal, when he wanted a lighter accompaniment, he would turn to us saying 'Miracle piano, miracle piano!' He always got a good balance.

There was also the advent of the young Daniel Barenboim. *Was he a major figure in the development of the ECO?* Yes, our management very correctly jumped on anyone who had a great talent and could fill the halls, but wasn't yet quite famous enough to be terribly

Kay Hurwitz

Mstislav Rostropovitch

expensive. I remember Barenboim showing us how Mozart, who used to direct from the keyboard, kept one hand free at important tutti entries. At a reception after a concert on the South Bank, Claudio Arrau, who had just played with another orchestra said 'Daniel, you're a wonderful boy, but you're really greedy—you want to do everything yourself. I think that a concerto is a dialogue between soloist and orchestra. How can you both play and conduct?' Barenboim replied 'When these works were first played, the same man played and directed them, and he'd also written them!' Arrau laughed—he had no answer to that.

The only time we used to quarrel with Barenboim was when he didn't want to do another take of something. *What was his reason for that?* He thought that a take was OK providing it had sufficient flair. I said to him that at his age he might be able to record these works perhaps three times in his life, but for us this was very important. He replied 'Don't be such an old woman!' One Wednesday we were booked to do two sessions to record the Mozart **Concertante** for four solo wind instruments. The next day was the Haydn **Sinfonia Concertante** for strings and wind. I was looking forward to the Wednesday night at home to polish the solo part. Arriving on Wednesday morning, we found that Barenboim had decided to do them the other way round, so we didn't have the practice time. *Why did he decide to do that?* I have an idea that one of the wind players had a slight problem with his lip and needed a day for recovery. *So did you feel less prepared when you came to do it?* Not really, but when I listen to that record I notice the odd note slightly out of tune. If I'd been listening more carefully to the playback I'd have asked to do some passages again. Generally I have found that in the playback room the volume is higher than I like, so I tend to listen from outside the room. Over the years my colleagues have learnt to indulge me in this eccentricity.

Did Ashkenazy conduct the orchestra? Ashkenazy totally refused to conduct in those days. We were performing many piano concertos with Barenboim and occasionally one with Ashkenazy, who would always say to me 'Please, you take care of the orchestra'. He didn't want to have anything to do with it.

I first heard Jacqueline du Pré when she was fifteen, at Cecil Aronowitz's house. Already she was a very complete player, although her technique at that time was based too much on fast bow strokes—the sound came gushing out. I didn't think she played into the string enough. The ECO accompanied her in Haydn concertos and I remember the tremendous gusto of her C major, and the sincere and passionate intensity in her recording of the D major. I also accompanied her in the Elgar Concerto with Barenboim—in this she was a great artist.

I am perhaps the only person who has played a concerto in the Carnegie Hall in New York for £15. I was playing the Mozart Sinfonia Concertante with my colleague Cecil Aronowitz. The management decided to increase both our fees to a concerto level. My fee as leader was more than his as principal viola, so I got a smaller increase—the £15.

When did Terence Weil leave the orchestra? It might have been in the early 1960s, which was when Keith Harvey took over. Keith had a very distinguished career in the orchestra and also played as soloist. *He told me a story about being on tour with you, playing the Haydn C Major Cello Concerto in South and Central America. This work has a very lively finale, and you'd give him a wink as, each evening, you would start it a notch faster.* Keith was a brilliant young player, having been principal cellist of the LPO at twenty—his first job after leaving the Royal Academy.

I played several concerts with Nadia Boulanger in which she conducted Brandenburg Concertos and some works of Stravinsky, including the Violin Concerto with Menuhin. *What was her conducting like?* By this time she had become obsessed with upbeats. Gareth Morris found it especially irritating in Brandenburg No. 5. We also did the Faure **Requiem** a few times with her. I remember her remonstrating with Cecil Aronowitz, our principal viola, saying 'Please try to sound like a choirboy—it is too romantic'. He was using a really luscious vibrato all the time. At the end of the rehearsal she said to him 'I would not marry you—you are too sensual!'

We did a lot of work over the years with Charles Mackerras. I remember an early BBC concert with the Goldsborough Orchestra. A tape of this particular broadcast was found recently. It included a Dance Suite by Bartok which I haven't heard played since, a very fine piece. Another visiting conductor was Colin Davies whom I first encountered as a clarinettist, playing in the Schubert Octet. Raymond Leppard worked with us regularly, often directing from the harpsichord.

How much, in the early days of the orchestra, did you work with Lawrence Leonard? He was my conducting teacher. We did a certain amount of work with him in the early years of the orchestra but eventually he decided to take his career more in a symphonic direction. *How do you remember him?* I remember Lawrence as a very talented young man. His father, who died in his forties, was the viola player of the Stratton String Quartet which later became the Aeolian. When **West Side Story** opened in London, in the late 1950s, Lawrence became the conductor of the show with the Goldsborough Orchestra. Nobody in England realised what a gold mine that show was going to be. *Did he conduct it for a long time?* Yes, for years. I was really very sorry that the management wouldn't allow me to play in the show. They felt it was bad for the orchestra's image if I were to take part. *Was it, effectively, an A orchestra.* Yes. Later on, in orchestral programmes, the ECO would often be out at two different places in one evening, but with the same name. It would be in one town with me leading, and in another with Ken Sillito leading.

One of the last things I did as a member of the ECO, was to go to lunch with the management of the orchestra and Imogen Holst, daughter of Gustav, who was a conductor and choral director. She was a musician of great sensitivity. When we were rehearsing a small Holst choral piece with orchestral accompaniment she said 'You must be particularly tender with this piece, because I was being conceived at the time it was being written'. She had always been a great stalwart of the Aldeburgh Festival and used to put all Britten's last minute changes into the scores of his works while they were being rehearsed. She was retiring from conducting in high dudgeon. Some critic had not liked a performance of hers, so she decided she'd had enough. As we had noticed that she wore a bedraggled old fur coat to winter concerts, we bought her a new one as a goodbye present. I've no idea whether it was real or mock fur, but when we gave it to her she said 'I'm really pleased, because I won't have to go on using mother's anymore. I had to keep putting tape on to hold it together.'

Were you in the ECO for Daniel Barenboim's Mozart piano concerto recordings? I was there at the beginning of them, but I'm not sure how many I did. There are a lot of these concertos—I must have done about twelve to fifteen. My successor, Kenneth Sillito, continued after I left. *What year did you leave the English Chamber Orchestra?* 1968. *That was a landmark for you and a change of direction?* Absolutely. The management wanted me to stay: they said I was merely having a mid-life crisis—after all I was nearly fifty.

When I left the ECO I knew that I could devote a few hours a week to teaching. Soon after, in 1969, I accepted a position at the Royal Academy of Music.

Although the Melos was busy in 1968, our pianist, Lamar Crowson, couldn't afford to live in England any more. He went to a very good job in South Africa.

* * * * *

In 1968 Jackie married artist and scenic designer Michael Minas, and her career in jewellery was developing splendidly. Our son Michael, then a teenager and not being particularly into practising, put his cello aside and took up the bass guitar. He started a group and was earning money from gigs when he was fourteen. This phase lasted for two years. Then he started to think about what direction his life should take and decided that, not having done much work at school, he was best at the cello. He took some lessons from Keith Harvey and later from Amaryllis Fleming. Some time after my mother's death in 1967, Michael went to live in her house in Stoke Newington. He never went to music college but just drifted into work. I suggested that he form a string quartet: in 1969 he met my pupil Adrian Levine, and the Amphion Quartet came into existence. Since the other three were at different music colleges, Michael made friends and contacts in each.

20

Conducting

In the early 1960s I had a series of lessons on the basic technique of conducting from Charles Mackerras. I had first met him at a party, soon after he had arrived from his native Australia. At the time he was playing oboe in the Sadlers Wells Opera, but he told me that he was looking forward to having a conducting career in England.

Did you get many conducting opportunities from the time you started? Yes, I did quite a lot of concerts with the ECO around the country. I led the orchestra for the Brandenburgs, and then conducted the other works. *How did that reflect in your pay packet?* I don't think it affected it at all. *But you told me once that you made much more money from conducting jobs?* Yes, I did when I conducted a BBC orchestra in Birmingham and Manchester, and several times in Scotland: I also conducted the London Mozart Players. I noticed that, even on a modest conducting date, I was paid very much more than when leading an orchestra. *Do you think that you were able to contribute more as an orchestral leader than as a conductor?* Yes, I felt more at home conducting small orchestras—I don't think that I conducted anything much bigger than the Brahms **Academic Festival Overture**. I felt that I could have directed small orchestras equally well from the violin in classical works, although not in the modern repertoire. I conducted the Beethoven and Brahms violin concertos with soloists I knew and also the Walton Cello Concerto for Amaryllis Fleming, with the Scottish Orchestra. I also conducted some concerts of Bach cantatas with the ECO.

I soon stopped using a baton. In my very early days of conducting I'd managed, a couple of times, to break one and fling it away. *Was this with displeasure?* No, just through bad technique. Once, in a rehearsal, I remember, while giving a violent beat, getting the baton caught underneath my glasses, which were flung into the orchestra. But when, one day, my baton broke in half and the top half fell on the leader's Stradivarius, I felt that it would be much better to be a

Less dangerous without a baton

little less clear, but not so much danger to people. *Was that recommended by your insurance broker?* Not exactly.

To what extent would you agree with the concept that conducting is a phoney profession? It is for bad conductors, but not for good ones. I remember that we'd often have conductors in the ECO who were not particularly distinguished. I'd always say to my colleagues that we section leaders, where necessary, must have a conspiracy of ensemble. However, in the Philharmonia, I found that I couldn't hold a whole symphony orchestra the way I could hold an orchestra of twenty-five or thirty—it was just too big, so some notice had to be taken of the conductor. *But what about the so called standard performances, that members of symphony orchestras say they have, to survive bad conductors?* Herman Scherchen said that it takes an excellent conductor to make a good orchestra sound better than usual, and an exceptionally bad one to make it sound worse. Once, on a date with a new conductor, I said to a principal wind player in the coffee break, 'I'm not terribly impressed with this man'. He answered 'I haven't looked yet.' *I once asked the distinguished principal bassoon player of a well-known chamber orchestra what their new conductor was like. He replied, in an amiable tone, 'Follows OK.'*

The cellist, Alfred Wallenstein, did a certain amount of conducting. He was ambitious and, while leading the Boston Symphony cello section, would sometimes look up and hiss in disapproval. One day, at the end of a rehearsal, Bruno Walter said 'My dear Mr. Wallenstein, I know that you have ambitions to conduct. The best thing that I can wish you is that, when you succeed, you won't have a Wallenstein playing principal cello.'

21

. . . .

Philharmonia

A few months after leaving the ECO, I joined the Philharmonia as co-leader. *Did you already know Otto Klemperer?* Yes. In his last years, ensemble was very difficult, because he conducted sitting down, having recently had major surgery: his conducting was reduced to a few gestures. *I remember seeing him at a rehearsal. To me, the Beethoven Symphonies seemed very slow. What was your feeling about that?* I found that Klemperer always kept moving in the Beethoven slow movements. They were sometimes a little faster than other conductors. It was the first movements, the scherzi and the last movements which tended to be heavier and slower. The Beethoven Symphonies may have seemed very slow compared to Toscanini. We tend to think that the first way we hear something, as a youngster, is the right way. It's hard to decide to do it any other way.

If you take the opposite polarities of Toscanini and Furtwängler, there are certain similarities and certain differences in their speeds, but I found that these last performances of Klemperer were extraordinarily slow. You must remember that he was a giant musical intellect but, physically, semi-incapacitated. I have a video of him conducting a Beethoven symphony in 1970, in which I was leading the Philharmonia. It was a programme sent to me by a Dutch student. At the end of this performance there was a discussion in Dutch about the tempi. Then they put on a film of Klemperer conducting Beethoven twenty years earlier. This had tremendous rhythmic virility and the tempi were quite a lot faster. When I came to the Philharmonia as leader, I found that some of the slow tempi were connected to the fact that, in this enormous orchestra, nobody wanted to be the first person to be ahead of the beat. *Do you think that Klemperer's perception was affected by his illness?* I think so. I remember that Enescu said 'As a man in my seventies, I want this music to be a little slower, to hear it vertically as well as horizontally.' *I think that there is a remark to that effect by Brahms.* In the Brahms Violin Concerto, and in the sonatas, there is sometimes the warning: Allegro ma non troppo. The **ma non troppos** were not put in by Brahms, but added by Joachim, who didn't want to play these movements too fast.

In 1970, the Philharmonia played in the Beethoven Bicentenary in Bonn. It was nearing the end of the year of celebrations and many famous orchestras had already taken part. We did the **Coriolan Overture** and then the **Eroica Symphony**—that was the entire concert. A press review said that it was the finest performance they'd heard in the whole year. I remember the pleasure of playing Beethoven, Bruckner and Mahler symphonies with Klemperer, but not liking at all his approach to Haydn or Mozart, because to me his slow tempi inhibited the flow of the music.

Lawrence Leonard told me that he once did a radio programme investigating Beethoven's metronome markings. He found that there were ten or so tempo indications in the symphonies that were just too fast to work well. My idea is that if we assume that Beethoven's metronome was fast by a certain percentage, and reduce the tempi by that amount, the markings might then indicate more playable speeds which are related to his intentions. Yes, that's possible. For a string quartet, the metronome mark of the finale of Beethoven's Opus 59 No. 3 is at an incredible speed. Bartok made a second edition of his own first string quartet. He said that he had to modify many of the original tempi because they were either far too slow or far too fast. He remembered that when, as a young man, he was writing something, he would play a section on the piano to see how many minutes and seconds it took. I've found, when working with Britten and Tippett, that distinguished composers can have a tendency, because they know their piece so well, to want tempi that are faster or slower than is practical.

Did you work much with Carlo Maria Guilini? Yes, he was a very fine musician with strong ideas. He made the orchestra sound sumptuous—perhaps Barbirolli and Stokowski were the only other conductors who had this ability. Guilini's performances of the Verdi **Requiem** and Beethoven's **Missa Solemnis** were majestic. If he had a fault, it was that his Mozart and Schubert were too romantic. He worked with the world's top orchestras and tended to accept them as they were. Once I asked for three or four goes at a passage and he said he was not accustomed to rehearse to improve technique. Originally a viola player, he tended to bring with him parts with his own bowings. On the whole they were excellent but, occasionally, I wasn't comfortable and would ask if we could bow something another way. He would take the parts back to the hotel with him and next day would agree. When he wanted the strings to play very softly he tended to put the notes of a whole bar or even more into one bow, virtually extinguishing the string sound.

I played Vivaldi's **Four Seasons** at the Festival Hall with him. Before our first rehearsal he said to me 'Remember, no ornamentation'. However, at the rehearsal I showed him a few ornaments that I wanted to do and he liked them. Unfortunately there was no review of this concert because of a Fleet Street strike. We did fewer concerts with Guilini than with Klemperer, but I remember how he produced warm-hearted, beautifully musical playing. He was one of those rare conductors who can help to make a good orchestra sound even better.

* * * * *

When the Philharmonia was in America, the first flute, Gareth Morris, was injured in a mugging outside the hotel, near the Lincoln Centre. We had to find another player for the last five concerts. Norman Knight, our second flute, took over, and we engaged a fine American flautist to play second. This player was paid his usual fee, which was more than I, as leader, was receiving. However, the people who got more money than either of us were the baggage handlers of the American Teamsters Union. The actual work was done by our own baggage people, who knew the correct way to load the instruments. The Americans just stood by. For this they were paid $150 a day.

My first visit to Japan was with the orchestra, on a tour conducted by John Pritchard. I remember two beautifully dressed little girls coming on to the platform, at the end of a concert, bearing wrapped gifts—a tiny one for the conductor and a somewhat larger one for me. Afterwards, before opening them, John said that he was entitled to the larger one and I was quite happy to swap—I still have the exquisitely cast miniature Japanese bronze bell, but I don't know for how long he kept his picture of Beethoven in a plastic frame.

I was quite horrified to find that, during my couple of years with the orchestra, we hardly ever did a Brahms or a Tchaikovsky symphony. This was the period when Mahler, Bruckner and Shostakovitch were becoming very popular. *Wasn't the reasoning that Mahler and Bruckner were still relative novelties and needed to be prominent in the programming?* I think that they'd come in already, just a few years earlier, in the mid 1960s. Sibelius had had a tremendous innings early in the century, as had Brahms.

In Constant Lambert's book, Music Ho, one chapter heading is **The Appalling Popularity of Music**. He complains that there was music in every restaurant and shop. Interestingly, in the 1930s, this music tended to be a Strauss waltz or a Beethoven symphony. It was before the advent of pop and jazz, which was only broadcast late at night. *In 1958, when I first went into the HMV shop in Oxford Street, the classical department was on the ground floor. If you wanted to buy a popular record, you went down a flight of stairs into the basement—now it is the reverse.* I remember being in shopping malls in the 1990s in Australia and seeing several of Richard Branson's Virgin shops. The pop music was being played terribly loudly. Occasionally I would remonstrate, but the manager would say 'It's the policy of the shop to do this.'

What made you decide to leave the Philharmonia after a couple of years? At that time, the management of the orchestra had decided that the image of the Philharmonia should be updated. Because it had done so much work with Klemperer, it was getting a rather heavy, stodgy approach to playing—not enough New York or Chicago accent. They appointed, as guest conductor, a young man called Lorin Maazel. I worked with him for a few months. He was quite a magnificent conductor, but I didn't particularly enjoy making music with him. I had liked very much working with the two principal conductors, Klemperer and Guilini, and we'd occasionally have a fine youngster like Colin Davies come in. Somehow, Maazel's way of making music was so different from mine that I felt it would be very difficult for me to do what he wanted. I used to be a very innocent leader of orchestras, not questioning the quality or the authority of a conductor but just trying to get the best results possible. *You learned your lesson in the war years?* At that time some of my colleagues would literally go to the ends of the earth to escape our bandmaster.

22

Aeolian Quartet

The Seventies was a more introspective decade. It saw the start of the environmental movement, the growth of feminism and generally a movement towards a more egalitarian society. The personal computer was marketed and there was the birth of the internet. It was an uncertain period for the economy in America and Europe but a time of rapid expansion for Japan.

For me it was also a time of change. In 1970, the leader of the Aeolian Quartet left the group rather abruptly at the start of the season. Sidney Humphreys, a very fine player who'd been with them for fourteen years, decided that he wanted to return to Canada. The quartet had been in existence since the 1930s, originally known as the Stratton Quartet, after its distinguished leader, George Stratton. It was renamed after the war. In seeking a new leader, the first person they asked was Manoug Parikian, who said that he wasn't interested.

It was a week when the Philharmonia wasn't working and I was leading a small orchestra in Croydon. Some of my colleagues asked if I were interested in the Aeolian job. I said at first that I wouldn't dream of doing it. However I knew the players in the quartet because they'd worked with me at various times in the ECO. Raymond Keenlyside then approached me personally, asking if I would help them out by by doing two rehearsals and a concert with them.

What made you decide to join the quartet? After rehearsing a couple of times with them I said 'I'll do my best to help with this season's work'. In the end there were only three concerts out of more than thirty that I could not play. I was helped in this by a very accommodating attitude from the Philharmonia. They let me off pretty well everything requested. At the time I was the official leader of the orchestra, because Carlos Villa, with whom I shared the job in my first year, had gone back to Columbia. I asked a friend and colleague, Raymond Cohen, a previous leader of the RPO, to help

Aeolian Quartet

me. He came in to share the work with me and played in quite a few of the concerts. I decided that I would join this quartet rather than work with a conductor who I didn't feel would be a comfortable boss.

A newspaper reporter asked me the reason for my decision. I answered that whereas some people are seduced by alcohol and others by drugs or women, for me, returning to this music made me feel like a sultan coming back to his harem after a long exile. The Haydn, Mozart, Beethoven, Schubert and Brahms quartets form an utterly incredible repertoire.

I'd played in virtually every other chamber music permutation in my years with the Melos Ensemble, but only occasionally did we play a string quartet. One instance was when Britten asked us to perform the Debussy Quartet at Aldeburgh. We also played it at the Edinburgh Festival. *How long did you remain in the Melos?* At the time of joining the quartet I decided that I could not continue with the ensemble. I was in the group from 1957 until 1970. By that time Lamar Crowson had left, and both Gervase de Peyer and Neill Sanders were leaving to work in the USA. My position was taken over by Hugh Maguire, a very fine violinist and musician who, over the years, had already played a number of concerts with the group.

I was happy to play with the quartet, because they were players with whom I could learn and who really extended me: I've always chosen colleagues who make me work quite hard. Raymond Keenlyside was ideal to play with. He had all the qualities of a fine leader but enjoyed being an inner voice. Margaret Major was always well prepared; the quartet benefited from the breadth and solidity of her playing. By contrast, I learnt my part in the rehearsal. Derek Simpson was a natural player with excellent tone production. He could pick up any cello and make it sound marvellous. I felt genuinely grateful that my colleagues had so much expertise.

I think a string quartet has two balances that are vital. The first is the balance of equal parts, with the second violin and viola equal to the first violin and cello. The second is the need for the players to speak the same language with comparable expression in each part. You can't have an impassioned violin phrase followed by a stolid one on the viola. Bernard Shaw once wrote in a review that when Joachim had a few bars rest in a quartet, everyone waited patiently for him to come in again.

The other three players in the quartet lived in South West London—I was the only North Londoner. We had long journeys back and forth along the North Circular Road for rehearsals. Sometimes, unthinkingly, I would find myself driving towards the Festival Hall in the morning, when I should have been heading towards Richmond. I always remember, when a rehearsal was at my house, how both Margaret and Raymond would arrive half an hour early in order to practise their parts. Derek was a natural player and the cello parts presented no problems for him, so he would enjoy a cup of coffee in the kitchen.

By the end of 1970 I was playing with the quartet virtually full time. It was unusual not to be playing in an orchestra. For years, I had become used to driving in the mornings to the Queen Elizabeth Hall with the ECO, or the Festival Hall with the Philharmonia. Suddenly, I had a less secure income. The quartet was doing well but, in comparison with my salary as leader of the Philharmonia, I had a financial shortfall at the end of the first year: I needed to find an extra two or three thousand pounds. I've always enjoyed collecting violin bows, and I remember with some anguish having to sell a couple of fine examples.

We toured Australia in 1970. Although I was still the nominal leader of the Philharmonia they let me out of all but one of the engagements. I told the quartet that I could do the whole six weeks in Australia, except for the last three days, when the concerts were in Brisbane and Cairns. One of the places I'd always wanted to visit was the Great Barrier Reef, so I felt very sad about missing the opportunity to see it. Two string trio concerts were substituted. It transpired that Guilini wanted me for a **Missa Solemnis** in the Swansea Festival, but I felt that Swansea was a pretty poor swap for the Barrier Reef. I didn't see it until 1992, when I went back to Australia to adjudicate in a new chamber music competition in Melbourne. The organisers were going to send me a business-class ticket, but I requested instead a couple of ordinary tourist tickets, so that I could take Kay with me on the trip.

When I left the Philharmonia, I announced that henceforth I'd be like a retired Sheriff in a Western, who would say that he was not going to pull out his gun any more. In those last few years I'd really become fed up with those distinguished conductors, especially of the ECO, who said that they must have me to lead. I argued that if someone's getting a few thousand pounds to conduct, they can't justify being dependent on a player who commands only a rather modest fee.

* * * * *

In 1972, we were contracted to record all the Haydn String Quartets. *How did the course of the quartet's activities change with this contract?* There are eighty-three Haydn quartets, mostly published in sets of six. Our schedule normally involved six days at St John Smith's Square to record a set. We were fortunate to have, from Robbins Landon, miniature scores of many of the quartets, which had markings added in three different colours. Black ones were from the manuscript, red were the markings made by Haydn's quartet at Esterhaza, who rehearsed with the composer; in green there was the occasional dynamic marking or slur that Haydn himself had added for the first edition.

The only early quartet that we already knew was the Serenade Op. 3 No.5. However, it was by then no longer politically correct to include it, because the musicologists had decided that it wasn't written by Haydn. On the plate of the set, Hofstetter's name had been rubbed out, and Haydn's superimposed. In those days, sonatas, quartets or trios were published in sets of six. If there were only four or five, a couple of pieces by another composer were put in to make up the set. The musicologists considered that this was the necessary evidence.

However, one of the musicologists, Reginald Barrett Ayres, co-editor of the new edition, broke ranks with his colleagues, because he considered that Hofstetter couldn't have written the Opus 3 Serenade. After spending a morning rehearsal playing through six or seven Hofstetter quartets we totally agreed with him. Decca wanted us to include an original Hofstetter Quartet to go on this same disc, as a comparison in style. These pieces were all totally amateurish: they were feeble harmonically, with lots of consecutive fifths and things which just didn't sound right. We decided that Hofstetter couldn't have written the Opus 3 Serenade—unless he'd had a flash of divine inspiration, which he'd never had again.

* * * * *

Did you go on many tours with the quartet? We travelled quite a lot, but not as much as we could have done. We never managed to get work in Japan, although our Haydn records were selling very well there. We played in Germany, Austria, Italy, France, Holland, quite often in Belgium and we even got to Cyprus. There were two big tours in Australia and New Zealand. We toured in South America and, in Chile, met the poet Pablo Neruda, who was later a Nobel Prize winner. A Soviet film crew were doing an interview with him. He seemed very comfortable, listening to our Haydn Quartet, with a Russian blonde sitting on his knee.

We didn't visit the USA, because we were very firm about how much money we wanted. By the 1970s the American agents were taking twenty per cent. When I went with the Melos, we had gone under the auspices of Sol Hurok. We made twice the money we were making in England at the time—fees tended to be higher in the USA.

We did a few recording sessions with Bing Crosby and Gracie Fields when their record company wanted some small-scale accompaniments. They were right on top of their repertoire and were pleasant and easy to work with.

In 1973 my friend, Jocelyn Selson, had visited a beautiful house in Monterosso, Italy, which she thought would be an ideal venue for a summer school. The lady owner also had several houses to let in the village. The first year we ran the school I went with the quartet to teach chamber music. I also conducted a string orchestra of thirty players, made up of students and amateurs. It was very successful but, in subsequent years, I only allowed full-time music students on the course. In 1979 we moved to another venue in Lerici.

In 1979 the quartet played in Iran just before the Shah was deposed, on a tour arranged by the British Council. In Isfahan we were suddenly moved to a cheaper hotel, because the Shah was coming to the town and wanted the whole of the best hotel for himself and his retinue. Another memory from this tour was seeing some unusual ceramic violins being played by local musicians.

In 1980 we toured in the Soviet Union. They insisted on our replacing the proposed Britten and Rawsthorne quartets with works by Shostakovitch. The concerts used announcers, rather than programmes. We finally got to play a Rawsthorne piece at the British Embassy in Moscow, a big city without any adverts, except for those of the Communist Party. The restaurants had live bands, rather loud, reminiscent of England in the 1930s. On our first free morning we visited the Kremlin. Our guide spoke good English: when we finished our tour I asked her where she would choose to have a holiday. She said, with misty eyes, that it was her dream to visit Disneyland, Florida.

How long did you stay with the quartet? In 1981 we mutually agreed to call it a day; I had played in it for the last eleven years. Within a fortnight of the quartet disbanding I found myself doing a certain amount of teaching. *Did you ever feel, after you finished the quartet, that you would have liked to have expanded your conducting career?* By the time I finished playing quartets I hadn't conducted much for several years—just the occasional Haydn or Mozart Symphony for a charity concert. Sometimes, when I had worked with youth orchestras, I enjoyed the rehearsals much more than the concerts. In the rehearsals one could be teaching and making the situation better. At the concerts I felt that, if I were leading the orchestra, I wouldn't need myself up on the rostrum.

In the late 1970s I had a letter from Buckingham Palace asking if I would accept a CBE. I had to look this up in the Encyclopaedia Britannica to see what it meant. A friend suggested that, in my case, it probably meant 'Collector of Bows Extraordinary'. It was fortunate for me that the custom of dressing up in a top hat had been discontinued the previous year—that wouldn't have suited me. I remember, at the ceremony, chatting with Peter Pears who was receiving a knighthood.

23

Diversion

A lot of the earliest string quartets have optional parts for two oboes and two horns. These are early divertimenti, which can be played either with or without the wind instruments. They might even have been played with more than one string player to a part, especially when they were played out of doors. In the Melos, we used to play three big divertimenti by Mozart: K334 in D, K287 in B flat, and K247 in F. These works are virtually violin concerti, although they are written as chamber music. They are scored for two violins, viola, bass and two horns. *Is one of these the Haffner Serenade?* No, that serenade is written for a normal orchestra—these are just divertimenti. Occasionally Toscanini would perform one of these, using the whole orchestra; Szigeti arranged one as a violin concerto, playing the first violin part alone. He used to perform it with chamber orchestras in the 1950s. In the violin part, these big divertimenti go right up to top D and E flat—several notes higher than Mozart's violin concertos. I loved playing them, because they are real virtuoso pieces for the first violin. There is a famous Minuet in the D major Divertimento that has a life of its own—it makes a good encore piece.

There's a catch question that I used to ask my pupils. 'Why are these works written for two violins, viola, bass, two horns but with no cello part?' To me the answer seems obvious—that Mozart wrote these pieces to be played at garden fetes, standing up. However, when we played them with the Melos, we used both cello and bass. *In the 18th century, basso continuo was the normal description of the bass line: don't you think that the manuscript could have followed that tradition?* I don't think so, because these works are already in the K250–300s, by which time Mozart had written many string quartets. He was very used to writing a separate cello part but, in all his concerti, the cello and bass parts have just one bass line in the score. *Perhaps this was for speed of writing?* There is no cellist on the title page of the set of parts of Mozart's Musical Joke. There

Eighteenth century engraving from the cover of Mozart's Musical Joke
(Courtesy William Waterhouse)

are two violinists, a violist, a bass player and, on the other side, the two horn players, wearing uniforms. Wind players were usually borrowed from the military band. There is no harpsichord player either.

There are certain spurious works that for a long time were politically correct. For example, the Violin Concerto K271A in D, supposedly by Mozart, which was often played in the 1940s, '50s and '60s—I remember both Grumiaux and Szeryng playing it. There's also a wonderful recording of it by the sixteen-year-old Menuhin, accompanied by Enescu. This work was always considered slightly dubious, because it went up higher than Mozart's normal range. Also, uncharacteristically, there were a couple of runs in tenths. It was probably put together in late Victorian times. There are a few rough 'tape joins', which don't have the smoothness of Mozart, especially in the last movement. I played this concerto several times, and broadcast it with Norman del Mar. I took out a few rather Victorian dominant sevenths, also the tenths in the violin part. My cadenza for the slow movement included the tenths, so that my colleagues wouldn't think that I couldn't play them. This work has not been played for about thirty years. If you listen to Menuhin's record, you'll hear that it is a very exciting piece; it has some of the most marvellous Mozartian writing that I've ever heard. There are many things in this concerto that parallel the music of the big divertimenti.

* * * * *

In the performance of chamber music, what qualities are needed by the leader of a group? In the old style quartet, if the first violin was off form it was a bad concert. In the new style, with equality of the four players, on a bad night for the first violin it can still be a good concert. Certainly, both the quartets I played in, the Hurwitz and the Aeolian, were of the more modern style.

Quantz, in the early 1700s, talks about the need for qualities of leadership. He describes playing in an orchestra with three different leaders. One of them he preferred, but he found it difficult to know why. A successful leader needs qualities similar to those of a good conductor. From the first note, the other players should feel musical authority emanate from the leader. This is the opposite of being hesitant or tentative, but neither should a leader be dictatorial. If the direction is good and natural, the other players will accept it with pleasure.

It is very important for a violinist, whether in chamber music or when leading an orchestra, to be able to play a line of sixteen semiquavers rhythmically. In concertos you may get away with waywardness, but not in chamber music. Very often a soloist hurries and expects to be followed. I remember leading a chamber orchestra for a very famous soloist who was directing **The Seasons**. There was a slight lack of ensemble, because the soloist wasn't playing as rhythmically as the orchestra. *Did you ask the soloist to follow you?* I discovered, as a teacher, that if you ask someone to play differently, they have to go away to think about it. It is difficult to make an immediate change. However, six violins sitting down, if playing together, can show a soloist that something is not working properly.

It is essential to develop the art of portraying the many moods of music. You may need a slightly different basic sound for different composers. For example, I wouldn't play a Mozart slow movement with the same basic tone quality as I would one by Brahms—it will need a different attitude to tone production. A quartet by Bartok or Hindemith will need yet another sound. No one player is best at every type of music, but some people are quite adaptable by nature. In chamber music, I've had few opportunities to make the sort of sounds one would make in a Wieniawski concerto. I have always relished making schmaltzier noises in Khatchaturian and Bartok, and in the Milhaud Trio with clarinet and piano.

Do styles of bowing need to be modified for chamber music? I first heard of Schmuel Askenase when he was in his early twenties, playing Paganini concertos. Two or three years later, not having enough solo dates, he found himself leading a quartet. Within a few weeks of practising classical string quartets, he found that there were a lot of bowings he hadn't encountered when playing Paganini. He was referring both to bowing styles and to the finesse required for the execution of certain passages in string quartets.

I remember once seeing Eli Goren leading a Haydn Quartet and was amazed by his exquisite bow control. It was on quite a small scale, an approach that would never be used by a soloist. When he led the BBC Symphony Orchestra, he played in a big style. By contrast, he said that he liked an economical style in chamber music, without flustery long bows. He played a lot in the middle of the bow, using it without gaps in the sound—legato rather than portato.

In the late 1970s at Aldeburgh, I played Mozart's **Concertone** for two violins with Menuhin. Britten asked him to join us in Brandenburg No.3. Menuhin said that it was a novelty for him to play sitting down. I was next to him, playing the second part, and was nearly blasted out of existence by the sound of his wonderful instrument. A violin heard from the back sounds more powerful. *Why then do players always face the audience?* Because from the back you hear more of the noises of tone production. Anyway, I couldn't imagine playing with my back to the audience.

24

The Eighties

The Eighties saw the end of the Cold War and the collapse of communism in Russia and Eastern Europe and this was when I received a piece of the Berlin wall in the post. There was much economic expansion—it was the time of the videocassette and the first mobile phones.

When I left the quartet in 1981 I felt that life was one long holiday. I was only sixty-two, but had been working continuously since 1946, often with three sessions a day, and endless touring. It was a great relief to be free of the constant stress of public performance. Only after three years did I start to miss giving regular concerts.

However, I remained fairly active. I played the Beethoven Concerto, a number of performances of the Brahms Double with Christopher Bunting, and of the Beethoven Triple in which we were joined by Joyce Riddell. There were also many performances of Bach, Vivaldi and Mozart concertos.

I gave a few sonata recitals with my friend Peter Wallfisch. In those years Peter was playing mainly cello recitals with his son Rafael. We performed Beethoven, Brahms and various Mozart sonatas. I'd played so few of these sonatas that it was a great luxury to do them, and I enjoyed this work.

It was good to be able to find the time to do some practice. I studied the C major Sonata of Bach—I'd taught the Solo Sonatas and Partitas, but had only performed the G minor, D minor and E major. I also learnt two fantasies that I hadn't played. They both did me a lot of good technically. One was the **Carmen Fantasy**—I think that the original Sarasate is better than the Waxman version. The other was the Schubert **Fantasy**, a great duo that was, in the past, not so often played. There are three very fine works for violin by Schubert: the others being the **Grand Duo** in A and the B minor **Rondo Brilliante**. The enormous set of variations written for flute or violin is usually left to flautists.

I don't think that I practised anything transcendentally difficult until I stopped playing seriously. Granville Jones, who was in my first string quartet, would quite often go off to play a concerto date. He would look at me innocently and say 'Don't you play these works too?' If you're playing a big concerto, there is the pleasure of being a racehorse. When, in March 1946, I was demobbed from the army I decided that there was little point in trying to become a soloist. I was nearly twenty-seven and hadn't practised since I was twenty—it would have been an unrealistic thing to do. Later, I found myself teaching works like the Tchaikovsky, Sibelius and Paganini concertos. I discovered, to my surprise, that there were very few difficulties which I hadn't experienced in Beethoven and Bartok string quartets. Thirds, sixths and octaves are the main difference, as these occur comparatively rarely in chamber music. Otherwise, the level of difficulty is similar.

When I was asked, in 1952, to play the Saint-Saëns **Rondo Capriccioso** with the Goldsborough Orchestra on a short tour of English towns, Eric Gruenberg was staying in our house. While I was practising this piece Eric said to me, 'You're playing it like a string quartet—let go of it.' He was quite right—I was being too controlled. *Did you then try to use more bow?* As a first step I practised making the accents more exciting. Also I made sure that I was continuing my bow between strokes. *Is this something more connected with a concerto style?* It is connected with a big style.

In playing a concerto, stamina can be a major element. Is it the same for a violinist in chamber music? I have found that the piece that I needed most stamina for was one I didn't play until I was in my early thirties—the Schubert Octet. There are six big movements, and it lasts almost an hour. That's a long time to be playing a work which is a semi-concerto. In both the violin and clarinet parts there are lots of difficult passages. And, of course, the art of playing with freedom while sitting down has to be cultivated.

I realised that I could have learnt the solos just as well as I had learnt the chamber works. My first concert, after I left the army, included the Ravel Piano Trio. Later, when teaching this work, I saw that a lot of young players with good techniques found certain passages in it quite difficult. When I was twenty-six I found no problems at all with it. *What specific difficulties did they encounter?* Playing the slow movement really softly and beautifully with very slow bows, and having a wonderful legato at either end of the bow. In my first few years after the army, most of my concentration was on learning to bow well. I wanted to find the magic of the bowing technique of Huberman, Heifetz and Kreisler—particularly very fast accents and wonderful slow bows.

25

. . . .

Teaching

When did you begin teaching as a serious, rather than occasional activity? During my time with ECO and the Melos there had been very little time available for teaching, because I was away for several months of the year. In 1969, after I left the ECO, I accepted a position at the Royal Academy, at first with just three or four pupils. However, when there was a lot of travelling it meant having to give pupils two lessons in a week. When I joined the quartet it was easier to coordinate activities, since Raymond Keenlyside and Margaret Major taught at the Royal College and Derek Simpson was head of the cello department at the Royal Academy.

In 1980, at the time the quartet disbanded, the remuneration at the RAM was dramatically improved. Suddenly good contracts were on offer. Fees were increased from £3 per hour to £25, so I expanded my class to ten or twelve students. However, in recent times, the pay in universities has fallen behind again. Professors are, on the whole, paid less than many school teachers. At a fairly recent meeting at the Academy, the Principal spoke about the loss of one of their top teachers, who had taken a job in America with a much higher salary.

Each year, three or four of my pupils graduated, and I had the luxury of auditioning about twenty applicants, so I could choose the students that I wanted. In addition, I usually had six to eight private pupils, so I was giving about twenty lessons a week. When teaching privately, there is often the need to accept pupils who can afford to pay, but I much enjoyed working with some young virtuosi who had studied at the Julliard School.

On two occasions I accepted students who had been thrown out by their previous teacher. He was annoyed because they were not practising their Paganini enough. *Was it because they were lazy?* No, they were more interested in chamber music, particularly in string quartets. I had a very good regime for both these young men. I asked them to practise certain first violin parts from Beethoven, Bartok and

Hindemith quartets, also the first two by Tippett—the only ones then written. There was a lot of technically challenging material for them to learn. *But couldn't it be argued that, if they had learned their Paganini caprices, they'd have played the chamber music better?* Absolutely, so long as they didn't spend too much time on such virtuoso works. *But had they spent sufficient time up till then?* I'm sure that they hadn't.

In a way somewhat similar to my departure from the Philharmonia, I eventually resigned my position at the Academy when a new head of strings was appointed. The Academy seemed gripped by an obsession with status. The aim was to increase this by going all out to produce an international soloist. I didn't wish to be directed by a young woman of twenty-three, even if world famous. She said that the violin teachers at the Academy were so old and out of touch that they hadn't got a clue about concert life and modern playing. I remember, when I left, a couple of my colleagues said that they felt the same way as I did, but they couldn't afford to leave. In the end that particular experiment was not successful, as the appointee said that the visits took up too much of her time, and so she decided not to continue.

Immediately after I'd left the Academy, I was asked to give regular master classes at the Royal Scottish Academy and went up there each month, for a couple of days. I was paid as much for that as for two weeks work at the Academy, because they were using their contingency fund. Their principal, Philip Ledger, I first knew as a young pianist who had occasionally replaced Lamar Crowson in the Melos Ensemble. I remember him virtually sight reading some of those difficult works, such as the Bartok Contrasts and the Shostakovitch Piano Quintet.

* * * * *

Can I now turn the tables and ask for your views on teaching as part of a playing career? *There are some aspects of teaching that modern thinking tends to skate over. A very fine performer is not necessarily a good teacher. A soloist may be a very natural, instinctive player, well taught from an early age. However, a teacher needs the ability to find solutions to a variety of problems. This is not magically acquired on receipt of a performance diploma—students have different needs and varying abilities. An analytical approach needs to be cultivated, along with communication skills, patience and diplomacy. Even with the desire to acquire such abilities, it can take a few years.*

Teaching needs to be more than a paid activity which conveniently supplements playing engagements—it is a skill that must be developed. As regards specific approaches to teaching, there are some teachers who concentrate more on technique, others on music. Without contact with both types, a student runs the risk of lack of balance. I think that Menuhin was right in saying that it is good for a student to go to a pedagogue for a certain length of time—one or two years, in order to learn technical discipline. The pedagogue is a person who is able to diagnose problems and explain how to overcome them—perhaps less talented as an executant, but with a capacity for analysis. In the end it is what a pupil understands that matters, but this comes from listening as well as explanation.

Some teachers are better at demonstrating than explaining, while others explain but don't demonstrate. Teaching is a good way of learning, because you have to be sure that you are doing what you teach. If you are playing concerts, your students can check on this.

Often teachers who don't play command a bigger fee than those who do. They can pontificate with so much more moral authority, not having the inconvenience of their playing being compared with that of anyone else. Joseph Fuchs, a successful virtuoso with a formidable technique, taught at the Julliard School. He became rather irritated because Ivan Galamian was getting, automatically, virtually all the great talent. He said he was convinced that a student learns more from a teacher who is, or has been, an executant. However, he waited till he was ninety before saying that.

26

Summer Schools

For how long did you continue your summer school in Italy? For fifteen years, from 1973–87. It ran from mid to late September, each year, just before the colleges started.

Around the time I left the Aeolian I happened to meet Neill Sanders, who had previously been the horn player in the Melos Ensemble. He had emigrated to the USA around 1970, because he felt the need for a bigger income. He went to Michigan University and started an ensemble there, similar to the Melos in London. He said 'I've got an excellent group of players, but they don't have enough experience of the main repertoire. Would you consider coming out to lead a little festival in the summer?' I thought that it was an attractive idea, so I accepted. I went back to playing Schubert's Octet, Beethoven's Septet, the Mozart and Brahms quintets, Bartok Contrasts and all those various pieces. These fine American players were working in the various universities in Michigan. It was most refreshing to perform this music with them.

Neill's Festival took place in a village between Grand Rapids and Kalamazoo, right in the middle of nowhere. Before I went there, the name only seemed connected with that well-known pop song 'I've got a girl in Kalamazoo'—now it turned out to be a real place. The hall was the renovated old village store, in a village called Shelbyville. They called it the Art Emporium. Neill and his wife Anne, a very good artist, had turned it into a concert hall that held two hundred people. They had a couple of millionaire patrons who provided a Steinway Grand and put some money into the venture. Anne's paintings and works of other artists were exhibited around the hall.

The summer temperature went up to thirty-five degrees. Anne and Neill lived in a cottage fifteen miles away, so I chose to stay in the Emporium to avoid early starts in that hot weather. However, I managed to keep fit with plenty of walking—I must have got to

Fontana

know most of the 'small dirt farmers' of the region. I went there regularly for several years until I was seventy, after which I said to Neill 'I think that now I'm old enough to retire from this summer job'. However, this group, which is called Fontana, has continued successfully to the present day.

I had been turning down invitations from summer schools in Germany, Sweden and Italy, where I would have been able to work in less terrible summer temperatures. At this time I was still playing seriously; not all that often, but with some really top class artists. *You were also teaching in various festivals, and giving courses and master classes in different countries?* Yes, I had my Italian summer school, and would occasionally work at courses in France and Germany, and quite a few in England.

I went on two occasions to a summer school in Sweg, Sweden, where I much enjoyed playing chamber music with Tibor de Machula, an exceptionally fine Hungarian cellist. He told me that, having married late in life and with a young daughter, he was cheerfully condemned to go on working for as long as possible. He was the first cellist of the Concertgebouw Orchestra and on a recent tour had played the solo in the Brahms B flat Piano Concerto in London. Since his Guarneri cello had been giving him problems, he decided to use on the tour the modest German cello on which he had begun his career. Nobody noticed, and the concert was very successful; but the Dutch violin dealer, Max Moller, made the observation that this was not at all good for the violin business.

Ten years ago I was asked to teach and play in the Yellow Barn Summer School in Putney, Vermont. It was quite a small gathering, with just forty or fifty students: at the time I was seventy-seven. I did courses there until only six years ago, when I found myself getting too tired to be able to rehearse and play concerts while doing a lot of teaching; I was playing with people whom I didn't know. Throughout my career, I have not enjoyed casually reading through works that I have performed professionally. On such occasions I found it more enjoyable to play viola. In my last year at this Festival, I played the Mozart and Brahms clarinet quintets with a virtuoso clarinettist, Charles Neidich, who taught at the Julliard. It was the first time I'd played the Mozart Quintet with the original basset clarinet.

27

Competitions

I didn't think that I would live long enough to see the collapse of the Soviet Union. Remember that I am of Russian extraction on both sides of my family. Later on, in 1997, I was pleased to see the return of a Labour government, because I thought that it was high time for a change. The previous administration had seen the rise of the yuppy, and I hadn't found the saying 'There is no such thing as society' very appropriate. I was glad to hear Tony Blair say 'We will govern with compassion', but before long I was disappointed because I found that this government was just as philistine as the previous towards the arts. An ever larger part of the country's resources seemed to be spent on administration. My view is that a country should ideally be as self-sufficient as possible. It is sad that we are not manufacturing so much steel, for example, but by now we have been priced out of the market.

In the Nineties I was still giving the odd concert and remember directing the London Mozart Players in the **Four Seasons**. I was doing quite a bit of private teaching, working at summer schools, examining at music colleges as an outside assessor, and adjudicating. I was one of the judges in the Carl Flesch Competition of 1990.

What are your general observations on adjudication? I've been on the jury of several international chamber music competitions, but only occasionally on international competitions for soloists, usually as a last minute replacement. I was at Menuhin's competition at Folkestone, and was the only chamber music player on the jury. One member had led symphony orchestras and a string quartet: the others were current or retired soloists.

When I complained about somebody's Bach, while on the jury of a competition, my colleague, a fine soloist, leant towards me and said ironically 'Manny, you must remember that we soloists are not as subtle as you chamber music players!' *Was this attitude apparent, in a collective way, amongst the reactions of the judges who were soloists?* Yes. However, six or eight judges quite often have different opinions,

Jury of the 1990 Flesch Competition, from left: Berl Senofsky, Emanuel Hurwitz, Ricardo Odnoposoff, Albert Frost, Ida Haendel, Zakhar Bron, Cicasch Tanaka, Devi Erlih, Herman Krebbers, Rodney Friend.

so it's a good thing that in the last few years adjudications have taken place without discussion. The markings go straight into a computer. In the past there was discussion and expression of likes and dislikes.

I remember an excellent fifteen-year-old being beaten by an unexceptional twenty-nine-year-old in a Carl Flesch Competition. Szigeti, coming on to announce the winner, looked slightly uncomfortable: it appeared that heads had been banged together in the jury room. Those were the days when there was discussion, and a charismatic teacher might sway other jury members. In the Flesch Competition the marks were recorded on the computer and the lowest and highest for each competitor were discounted. The reasoning was that, if a player received ten out of a hundred, there might be a bias against that style of playing; if ninety-five it might be a pupil of that adjudicator. In some competitions, judges announce when they have a pupil entered; the chairman did this when I was on a jury in Italy. I have known colleagues on international juries have their own personal scale of one to a hundred for seven or eight different points—things like intonation, shifting and tone production. A colleague once said to me 'I'm voting for X because she has eighty-seven points on my scale, although I found her playing very boring.

On one occasion the chairman of the jury, a famous soloist, wanted to give first prize to our choice for second place, leaving our winner second prize. We pointed out that he had only come on the day to hear the concerto. During the week, playing Bach, Mozart and Paganini, our winner had the best average. On the day, the other contestant played a marginally better concerto. The chairman said that we must accept his choice of the more exciting player: partly to please the patrons of the competition who were lay people. *What happened?* At the final concert we had them both play. *Who won the competition?* The all-round player—we managed to prevail.

A few years ago I gave a young man some lessons before an international competition. He was very gifted in his playing of Ravel's **Tzigane** and in two Paganini caprices. However his Bach G minor Solo Sonata was questionable musically; ugly mixed bowings had been put in just for comfort. When I suggested changes in the Bach he replied 'I've got to do it that way, because my teacher is on the jury!'

We know that competitors are often very unadventurous in preparing for competitions, for fear of offending one of the adjudicators; but how do judges hunt as a pack in selecting a winner? The first thing they demand is total technical security—if you don't have this, you're out. *After that, are there some plus points?* Usually there is solo Bach and Mozart in the early rounds—I have found that the important soloists on the panel usually discount these. *As things of little consequence?* Yes, they are waiting for the Olympic Games style of music. *Somebody who can stand up and dish out the goods—they are less concerned about the patterns on the china?* Yes. As a chamber music player, I know that most of these soloists are not themselves particularly good at Mozart concertos, or artistically convincing in solo Bach.

Standards have gone up a lot in the last forty years. Previously there may have been two technically outstanding players out of fifty, today there might be thirty-five. I've been on juries which start with the blind auditioning of tapes to decide who will be heard. In the Flesch Competition one jury member walked out, because one of his pupils hadn't passed the tape audition. By contrast, Ruggiero Ricci was rather amused when an arrogant young pupil of his failed to qualify: he was perfectly happy to continue.

I remember a clash of two judges in the Flesch Competition, Ricardo Odnoposoff and Berl Senofsky, both excellent violinists. We looked down the programme and it said that Odnoposoff had won the big 1937 Ysaÿe Competition in Brussels, whereas in reality we knew that he had come second to David Oistrakh. In that competition, while Odnoposoff had to lead the orchestra in Vienna only the previous night, Oistrakh had arrived with his entourage a week before. He had spent half a year preparing, having had a number of performances of the repertoire arranged by the state. Senofsky felt indignant about Odnoposoff's misinformation, having himself been the first American winner of that prize. Whenever Odnoposoff said anything, immediately Senofsky trumped it. I felt sorry for Odnoposoff, a small man who at lunchtime was being bullied by his much larger colleague; so I asked him if he had seen the article that Carl Flesch had written in the Strad magazine about the 1937 competition. He had written that Odnoposoff was quite the equal of Oistrakh. As he hadn't seen it, I copied it for him. Later I discovered that Odnoposoff had been a pupil of Flesch! *And so it goes on and on.* Yes. *My father attended that 1937 competition and was amazed by Oistrakh, whom he was hearing for the first time.*

I remember, in 1967, being told by a German violinist that the only ways to make a career were either to win an international competition or give money to an agent. I've never heard of giving money to an agent, but it is true that if they have influence they can get you a very good first season. But you're only going to be asked back if you're really successful as an artist. I've known of some players having their careers held back because their personalities clashed with certain important people at the top. *Many years ago, the day before the start of a European competition, my pianist cousin heard a competitor being coached by her teacher, a member of the jury. The girl just could not play a passage so, a moment before she reached it in the competition, the teacher dropped her pencil with a clatter. As the gallant jurymen scrambled to retrieve it, the passage passed unnoticed.*

* * * * *

How much does this need for technical perfection in solo playing apply in string quartet competitions? In the same way adjudicators don't like things being scratchy, not together or out of tune. However, I find that chamber music juries are always hoping to be given some artistic and musical pleasure. I've managed to prevail on several juries, and have never been asked back again, because I've gone against the consensus—but I've always enjoyed being a minority vote. *Was it because you were voting for the player or group with greater musical profundity?* Yes. *Whereas the others were looking for something more exciting?* In every generation you'll always get certain groups who play their Finales too fast, but I don't go for this approach. *Even Furtwängler has been known to do this—sometimes he seems to go berserk.* He's trying to be more exciting. *What does exciting really mean, because there's always the possibility of overkill?* I remember that once a quartet played their Finale so fast that Berlinsky, of the Borodin Quartet, leaned over and said to me 'Hysterich!'

I was once very pleased that my opinion about a group, which hadn't won, was shared by two members of the jury. One of them was Mischa Schneider, the cellist of the Budapest Quartet, and the other was the artist in residence there, Zoltán Székely, leader of the Hungarian Quartet. When an American group played the last movement of Bartok No. 4 ridiculously fast, Székely said 'When I played this, I'd learnt the notes. They're playing so fast that you just don't know if they have'. Milstein always preached, 'Don't play anything too fast. Just play rhythmically and cleanly and it will sound fast enough.'

In a quartet competition, one of the judges who was the editor of a new edition, was furious when a group played the work from the old edition which did not have his urtext changes: so, for him, that group was out. Often, in a masterclass, students who don't use the edition of the teacher are torn to pieces. Rostal always demanded that students used his bowings and fingerings when playing Beethoven Sonatas in his masterclasses.

A player I know, on the jury of a chamber music competition, was almost attacked in the street for not giving the first prize to a certain quartet. The group had a way of playing that was showy but superficial: they managed to get the audience on their side, so there was much public dissent. The accusation was 'Do you realise that you have ruined their career!' Perhaps they didn't see that you are bound to 'ruin careers' simply by making a choice. Yes, I've sometimes virtually been attacked by mothers of contestants. However, a career is not necessarily spoilt, because someone who isn't placed first may make the bigger impact later on. *I remember that Andras Schiff came fourth in the Leeds Piano Competition.*

* * * * *

A few years ago, in a competition for under-eighteens, I had to choose, from thirty-five recordings, ten players to take part in a masterclass in the Purcell Room. When giving the class, I listened to a number of violinists aged fourteen to sixteen. At one point I knew that the next person was due to play the first Paganini Concerto; looking around I couldn't see who it was going to be. Then I noticed that someone was trying to attract my attention by tugging at my sleeve: it was a small boy of ten—I hadn't thought of looking that low down!

How did he play? He has quite a remarkable talent—now he is in his early twenties and getting a number of international engagements. At his final college exam I heard his Mendelssohn first movement, which sounded as if it were being played by a computer—quite marvellous playing, but very square and cold. Afterwards, I asked him if he listened to Heifetz. He said that Heifetz's playing sounded messy. More recently I heard him again and it was vastly more musical.

This is connected with the fashion, between ten and twenty years ago, for playing with as many extensions as possible, thus eliminating slides. *I was told by my teachers in England that there had been a similar fashion in the 1930s—a reaction against previous times. Were you conscious of that?* No, I wasn't aware of this tendency or, if I was, I couldn't have found such players particularly interesting. In the 1930s I was listening to people like Kreisler, Heifetz and Elman who did various portamenti. That was still expected in performance.

You mentioned the Mendelssohn sounding like a computer. To what extent might competition entrants consciously limit their imagination and interpretation for fear of upsetting one of the judges? I've experienced a good string quartet sounding rather tame musically in a competition. I discovered, when they came to a chamber music course only a few weeks later, that they had toned down their rubatos and sforzandi in case the judges found them too way-out.

Would really first-rate musicians do that? In a recent Strad magazine article, there is an interview with Tabea Zimmermann, whom I consider one of the best viola players I've heard. She's talking about adjudicating in competitions, and thinks winning can be just the luck of the draw—who happens to be on a particular jury. She has had pupils ask if it is all right to do certain portamenti or rubatos in a competition, and always advises them that they will do best by just being honest and being themselves. She is very liberal, encouraging people to play their own way.

As a teacher at the Royal Academy, I had very few pupils aspiring to the level of international competitions. *Why?* Perhaps it is part of an English heritage of non-specialisation, which is now disappearing. I used to play in the orchestra of Dr. Reginald Jacques, who said that during the war he was on the jury for CEMA which arranged concerts for the troops during the war. Lots of young players used to come to audition for them. Just occasionally, a young violinist would perform some Wieniawski superbly. His colleagues on the board would look at each other nervously, because it was not the sort of music and playing they liked—just not quite British. *This was rather like Carl Flesch speaking about the reaction to Kreisler in the early 1900s.* When I went to the Academy in 1933, the teachers said 'We are not encouraging people to be virtuosi—we want them to be good, rounded musicians'. If you were a violinist, they wanted you to be able to play the piano quite well and also to be able to do some composition and arranging.

In England we still have had very few international level violinists, whereas we have had some fine cellists and pianists. An exception in recent times has been Kennedy. *Did you know Ralph Holmes?* Yes, he was a splendid player. *I couldn't understand why he didn't go further.* I think it was automatically difficult for an English person to be considered an international soloist. It also took a long time for English string quartets to be accepted in America.

After your long experience, are you less easily impressed than most other listeners? In the concertos of Beethoven and Brahms I have not heard, in the last fifty years, performances to compare with those of Kreisler, Szigeti or Huberman. I've often found the performances of some players pretty well juvenile. *Why is the element of profundity neglected in teaching nowadays?* Because the majority of teachers are not profound musicians. They are not particularly well versed in the great classical works and tend to pass on their own ignorance to their students. I am often really surprised when violinists, who have studied with great teachers, come to me for the odd lesson. I find that many points of phrasing they don't know about at all.

One of the most important things a teacher can do is to get the student to listen to major performers, both in concert and on recordings. Yet I know famous teachers who discourage comparative listening!

28

. . . .

Violins and Bows

From my childhood I have always had a great love of instruments. I remember, when I was about ten, a violin of one of my father's friends: a lovely shiny dark red fiddle. It was labelled Anselmo Bellosio, but was probably a French fake.

Choosing a good violin is not easy. I remember rejecting most of the ones that I tried in my student days. From the age of ten I played a very strong, loud French violin. It was a Collin-Mezin of 1926, which cost £8 in 1929. I liked its immediacy of sound, but didn't realise that tone quality also needs to be assessed from a distance.

Some time ago, a top violin expert said to Isaac Stern that it was becoming really difficult for a young player to find the large sum of money necessary to buy a fine old violin. Stern replied that he liked his pupils to use good modern instruments, on which they have to learn to produce their sound. I very much agree with that.

Is it better for a player to learn sound production on a modest instrument, rather than on a fine old Italian? It is all right to play on a modest instrument, so long as it has resonance and tone quality. Today I find quite a number of fine makers are producing instruments with an excellent sound.

When I was sixteen, a fellow student at the Academy went to Hills to choose a violin. He'd been told by his teacher to look for a Gagliano, Testore or Grancino. They would have cost around £100 at the time. However, he chose a Rocca of 1860 which cost just as much. He thought it sounded the best, but we regarded the choice, of what was then a modern Italian, as rather strange.

Today a Gagliano, Testore or Grancino will cost around £100,000, a Rocca or Pressenda £150,000 to £180,000. These makers are now considered more desirable. *Why?* The violins that have soared in price on the market are the louder ones. For example, the violins by J.B. Guadagnini, which are on the whole really strong sounding, cost more than those by some members of the Guarneri family. You can compare a dozen violins by del Gesu, Stradivari and

Guadagnini and they are liable to sound quite different from each other. Some are dark sounding, some medium and some bright. I find the sound of the G string on Pinchas Zuckerman's del Gesu wonderful, but it almost belongs to another instrument. It has three bright strings and a virtually viola quality G string, which I'm sure he loves.

I always liked a strong sounding violin. When playing with a nine foot grand piano, or with wind instruments, it is essential. *As regards volume, not many of the old Italian makers used the flatter model.* If you look at a great Strad or del Gesu you'll see that it is only flatter up to a point. If you want to see a really flat violin, look at a French copy. *Why are the Roccas so loud?* Because of the wonderful wood that he chose; he made very fine Strad and del Gesu copies. *I suppose that Vuillaume is the French equivalent.* Vuillaumes were incredibly expensive in the 1930s—they cost £80 to £100.

If you find a modestly priced violin or bow that works well, consider yourself lucky that you can equip yourself without being financially crippled.

I had a friend who knew all about wine. He said that normally he wouldn't dream of drinking a really expensive bottle. Some people want to spend that sort of money, but a connoisseur is looking for more modest wines that taste really good.

In 1966 I gave £250 for an Augusto Pollastri with a very special sound. A dealer friend said that I needed my head examined. Today they cost upwards of £35,000. The violin was lent to one of my pupils who is now using it to lead his very successful piano trio.

I knew a girl who, on leaving music college, had to return a borrowed Gofriller violin. She bought a new instrument by a very successful young maker and was really thrilled to find how well it worked. She went back to Canada and has used it in a successful career.

I've tried many Strads, and I remember certain violins with qualities so fantastic that I'll never forget their sound. However, I was always extremely happy with the brothers Amati that I played.

* * * * *

A player needs a feeling of safety in the bow arm. This brings eighty per cent of the confidence of any good violinist. There are players who develop wonderful left hands but have a little bit of stiffness or lack of comfort in their bow arm. In a concert this is magnified many times. There is no doubt that there are certain bows that stay like a railway train on the tracks. However I've found that, except for some of the greatest bows by Tourte, Peccatte and other great French makers, they don't usually work like that. You can look at a bow and there's a perfectly even sound coming out, but you can see the stick wobbling.

Another thing is that many young players play more on the side of the hair. When the bow is not very strong in the middle, the wood can scrape on the string. That is why student bows are always made just that little bit tougher and thicker in the centre. To play with a top-class French bow, you need the bow slightly more upright.

There has been a movement towards the use of stronger bows during the last century. Galamian, in the early 1960s, used to buy some excellently made bows in Switzerland, from the Finkel factory. He would hand them out to students who needed a bow. Many of them had silver lapping, which adds three or four grams, bringing the weight to 63–66 grams. 66 grams is already the weight of a light viola bow. Once you're playing on a bow of that strength and massiveness, one weighing 59–60 grams feels like a featherweight. I also bought some Finkel bows for my own pupils. They were priced at £8–£10 apiece and played as well as bows costing a lot more.

The violinist Sergio Luca, at a violin symposium in the USA, asked how many years it takes an ex-pupil of Galamian to appreciate a good bow. In those days, I had several players from the USA come to me for the odd lesson before a concerto. I found that some were playing with bows that weighed about sixty-five grams. Really a good bow shouldn't weigh that much—it can crush the sound of a fine violin.

I remember Daniel Barenboim bringing a young man of nineteen to my house after a concert: his name was Itzhak Perlman. He knew that I collected bows and wanted to try some. I got a box out and asked what kind of bow he wanted to try. He answered 'Gimme a club,' being used to a sixty-six gram bow. He spent an hour trying them and became interested in the subject. By the time he left London, a few weeks later, he had bought a Peccatte and a Voirin from Beare's—both very fine bows. He was an exceptional young man.

When a bow has both strength and flexibility, a violinist with the technical equipment can produce many types of spiccato. A spiccato can be anything from just off the string to a vicious little bounce. Bows which are strong and safe in the centre usually have only got one or two varieties of bounce, but many players seem to be happy with this.

Nowadays, the most sought-after bow of the last century is a Sartory, a maker already successful in the 1890s, who lived until 1946. His German assistant, Hoyer, suggested that if Sartory made his bows a little tougher, they would sell all over the world, not only in France. Two or three years after this, Sartory became the most popular maker in Paris.

In 1933, when I went to the Royal Academy, my teacher said that I should have a better bow. I tried French bows by Lamy, Voirin and Sartory, but I chose a Nürnberger, which was the sort of strong stick I was accustomed to.

Before the war, the cheapest Hill bow cost £1–£1 10s (£1.50). There were also lots of excellent German bows at this price, all made from very good wood. When somebody had saved up a few pounds they would usually buy a French bow. Many of these were too wobbly in the middle—they didn't have the solidity of a good Hill or Nürnberger. A good Hill has so much solidity that it feels as if it's running on railway lines.

I once bought a very fine Hill bow which was exceptionally heavy; I really enjoyed its solidity. However, I realised, after playing on it for a few days, that it made my other bows feel a bit flimsy. I decided to relinquish this one, so as to be able to enjoy the others.

Kreisler used to buy quite a few gold and tortoiseshell Hill bows which he sold to his amateur friends. This was to get a few dollars for card games, because his wife was very severe and rationed his money. Any bow which was ex-Kreisler sold well, so it was fairly easy for him to make a profit.

29

The Present Decade

I wondered whether I would live long enough to see in the Millennium. I remember seeing the Queen and Tony Blair on television, at the opening of the Dome, and found it extraordinary to be watching this.

It is hard to compare the troubles of the present decade with earlier times. As the Second World War was approaching, the nature of the danger was very clear—although the government of the time had taken a long time to wake up to it. Nowadays the dangers from terrorism are more uncertain. I miss the optimism of the post-war years.

I still give lessons: sometimes I help young violinists who are going to play a concerto in the Festival Hall—I'm very glad to work with them on something like that. The occasions when I get several good customers is when one of the orchestras has a vacancy for leader, or co-leader. People then come to me to play their compulsory solos: **Scheherazade**, **Zarathustra** and **Heldenleben**, and they also play me odd bits of Mozart symphonies. I'm pretty well the only experienced teacher who has led an orchestra and played these solos.

A number of people found that it was not possible to study with me because the grants that they'd received stipulated somebody who was teaching at one of the colleges. So there are not many people who now take advantage of what I can offer.

Kay continues to play, enjoying teaching and quartet playing and also, more recently, painting. Jackie has become rather famous for her jewellery design. Her daughter, Miraphora Mina, is also well known as a concept artist and graphic designer. She has worked in several of the major feature films of recent times. Now Mira's five-year-old son, Luca Caruso, has started at the YMC and is very enthusiastic about his music. The YMC has now about two hundred students, mostly string players. There are four orchestras, both a junior and a senior choir and a lot of chamber music activity.

Alec Lessin

A fairly recent photo

Michael played for many years with the Amphion Quartet and was Professor at Trinity College of Music. Now he is a member of the Philharmonia Orchestra. His wife, Miriam Keogh, is head of harp studies at the Junior Royal Academy of Music and a fine player. They have two sons: Alex who is a fitness instructor and Raphael who plays viola, piano and percussion.

I'm now a little wobbly on my pins. I began to feel somewhat older about three years ago when my sense of balance deteriorated. I no longer feel comfortable walking on to a platform. In recent years I conducted several concerts sitting down. *But you still exercise regularly?* I have to go for a smart walk in the evening to justify, as a diabetic, eating a meal. I also swim two or three times a week.

I remember that Joseph Fuchs, a senior friend of mine who taught at the Julliard, lived to be ninety-six. They say that in his nineties he still used to chase girls, but more slowly. Every year he gave a recital. When he was ninety, someone asked him 'What will you be performing?' He said 'That's not important—it's the fact that I'm playing at all that matters!'

This year you celebrated your eighty-seventh birthday: we can end by saying that yours is still an ongoing story. As long as I can show someone how to play a violin more easily, or to phrase more beautifully, I will continue. When you become comparatively old, being helpful and useful is one of the few pleasures left.

The next decade will be the Tens which, I remember, is where the story began . . . let's turn our attention now to the more important subject of violin technique.

The Knacks of Talent

Essential points of violin technique

Paganini's signature

Introduction

I teach pupils what I call the knacks of talent—abilities which give an audience the impression that you are a fine violinist. They are unconscious skills that bring about a liquid continuity in the left hand and arm when shifting, fine tone production in any part of the bow, and ease in any type of string crossing.

Those qualities we don't possess naturally we must learn, because our all-round progress is dependent on it.

The various virtuosi hold the violin and bow in different ways and, mentally, they have different priorities. Nearly every good player finds that some aspects of technique come more easily than others. Great virtuosi work out their own ways of overcoming technical difficulties, and the way they do this becomes part of their individuality. It is clear that everyone has to form their own technique.

Szigeti was a natural musician who talked a lot about details of technique and ways of doing things. He told me that, while preparing for publication a new edition of the Brahms Concerto, he discovered a fingering that facilitated a passage. A few days later he showed it to a young virtuoso who was visiting him. She tried it and said 'But, uncle Joska, I didn't find the other fingering difficult!' Szigeti then realised that he had only solved his own problem.

By contrast, Szerying was a naturally gifted technician who talked mainly about matters of musical interpretation.

From my early days of playing I had a strong sound, a brilliant trill and an instinct for knowing where I was on the fingerboard. When I was thirteen I looked at 'Le Ronde des Lutins' by Bazzini and found I could play immediately the middle theme—four F sharps, one on each string. On the other hand certain types of string crossing gave me problems for quite a few years. I also had to learn a good vibrato, which served me well till I was seventy. Then, over the next few years, it gradually became slower and didn't work so well. We tend to lose sooner those parts of our technique which don't come so naturally.

All players have to learn to make physical adjustments, modifying their technique to find what will work better. If there is something that we can't learn easily, the problem may be connected with tension in another part of the body. One day in a rehearsal, while leading the Melos Ensemble, I was having difficulty with a passage that was no trouble at home. I then realised that this was because I had practised it standing up. Being seated somehow complicated it. As a result of this, I had to learn a better-balanced sitting position. This was helpful later on when advising orchestral players who were uncomfortable sitting for long periods.

* * * * *

The first thing I establish with a pupil is general posture and a good, balanced way of holding the violin—this is of the greatest importance. It can take weeks or even months of experiment. Then we discuss how to change position without any audible connecting slides. Also essential is a good vibrato; this only works successfully when the left hand is free.

Freedom of the left hand depends to a great extent on the infinitely changing relationship between the thumb and the fingers. I have included in this section some exercises based on the need for flexibility and balance in the left hand.

Good bow distribution is an important factor in finding freedom of bowing. This is a subject that is strangely neglected, considering that it is a fundamental element of phrasing.

The two hands are interdependent: to have both arms operating freely is of vital importance.

If there is a stiffness in the bow arm, it will affect the left hand and the same is true in reverse.

* * * * *

To learn to project in public is perhaps the most important aspect of being a successful performer. Milstein said that if you use energy it breeds energy. Great players, however much energy they might be using, don't look physically uncomfortable or strained.

Huberman told me that he maintained one hundred per cent concentration while practising, thus getting into the habit of using himself physically. As far back as I can remember, I never wanted to play a single note on the violin that hadn't got quality of sound. I always sought tonal beauty and clean articulation. By listening for this all the time I found that practising didn't tire me.

Some violinists of considerable artistic talent may play well with a faulty technique but, in these cases, problems tend to start creeping in when they are around thirty-five or forty. At such a time they need the courage to be prepared to revise their technical approach.

I wasn't really aware of how to teach basic freedom of movement until I saw, in the mid 1970s, the ten short films by Paul Rolland. I realised that he was demonstrating the basic truths of how to play. On seeing these films, several of my distinguished colleagues were embarrassed by their own lack of awareness.

Posture

When playing well, with the body balanced and comfortable, the physical effort need not be enormous.

Playing an instrument can be compared to the use of the body in a sporting activity.

Playing a violin or viola is not a very natural position for the human body. The violin and the flute are the only two instruments in which the arms are held above the level of the heart, so the circulation has to be working well.

Some players fling themselves all over the place in the search for bodily and artistic freedom—this may be an excess of energy. I have always found that this excessive movement, though currently fashionable in some circles, is not helpful for optimum technical control. Great players tend to be self-contained dynamos.

A violinist with a fine talent may be doing several things incorrectly and still play well. Another player may do things correctly but not sound good. There are harder and easier ways of doing things.

* * * * *

The arms hover, as they neutralise the force of gravity. When playing the violin, the arms should be floating—there should be a total freedom in the arm and shoulder joints. This freedom in the arms and, indeed, in the whole upper part of the body, is the great challenge for the violinist.

Relaxation is a misleading term—a misunderstanding of it can lead to floppiness. Our muscles are organised in pairs: undue tension is caused by the contraction of muscles in opposition to each other.

Be careful not to overarch the back while playing, as this tends to encourage a flimsy tone production. This is a common fault amongst violinists—most don't know they are doing it.

If there is any stiffness in the bowing action, it tends to pull the body to the right on the down bow and to the left on the up bow. A test for this is to bow vigorously without moving the scroll. Another exercise is to stand on tiptoe while playing—for this, good balance is needed.

Technical Security and the Shoulder Rest

I knew a distinguished teacher who wouldn't accept any pupil who used a shoulder rest. He said that it prevented one from learning how to balance the violin properly; also from using the left thumb in a flexible way to help the hand move around the fingerboard.

Nearly all of my pupils at the Royal Academy used a shoulder rest. I didn't interfere, but insisted on their practising without it for a few minutes every day. This helps to develop the sense of the thumb acting as a pivot, for moving upwards and downwards.

Many problems in the right arm and left hand are caused by the relative inefficiency and stiffness of the thumbs. Once there is reliance on a shoulder rest, you can hold on to the violin much more easily. The shoulder rest tends to fix the violin more firmly in place. Then you don't need the left thumb as much to balance the violin or in downward shifting. However, if the left thumb is not used sufficiently, the hand becomes less sensitive to the problems of balance in playing.

Temianka said that in master classes he very often observed that students were not playing as well as they could, because they were not using either thumb correctly.

Joachim said that the thumbs of a violinist should function as intelligently as those of a pianist.

During an intense period of practice after the war, I encountered a problem in holding the violin, which I found rather puzzling. This was before the shoulder rest became popular. I experimented with many different types of pads and chin rests. Meanwhile, I was practising scales and arpeggios for a couple of hours a day. One day, I started playing and found that I was comfortable again. With all this work, my playing was improving, and I discovered that the greater efficiency of my left hand made me less reliant on the grip of the chin when shifting. Then I found that I could play with any of the various chin rests I had tried, but I decided to keep the original one. I had solved my problem unwittingly because, after two months of practice, my hand was now in much better physical shape.

A little later I experimented with the newly-designed shoulder rest, but found that it didn't help me. After a couple of weeks I wasn't playing as well. I noticed that it made the function of my left hand a bit lazier.

A shoulder rest can be a really useful device for supporting the violin if you can keep your left shoulder free while using it. However, if the shoulder joint is not free, it can bring about a less fluid left-hand mechanism: it can also affect the function of the bow arm, because the two sides of the body are interconnected.

To give a lead to other players, both arms must be free from the shoulder joint. However, when using a shoulder rest, holding the violin comfortably can effectively mean being locked into one position. Then, when giving a lead, you have to move from the waist, which is a rather cumbersome movement. Nevertheless some players of fine talent use a shoulder rest, and they are as elastic in their arms and shoulders as those playing without one.

If the violin is held in place, instead of balanced, you lose sensitivity. If using a pad, there is the need to make the violin go slightly uphill when you come down from a higher position. If you slide straight along, the instrument might slip away.

I remember being shocked when Menuhin first recommended his own model shoulder rest. Years later I asked him how long he had continued to use it. He answered 'Less than a year'. At the Menuhin School, the students were using them all the time. In many places, children as young as five are being given shoulder rests which are often too big for them.

Paul Rolland was the most outstanding teacher for helping young people to play without tension. He recommended the use of a pad of one, two or three layers of foam rubber, held on with elastic bands.

I use a little envelope of chamois leather; this is good because it doesn't slip. According to what I am wearing, I will put one or two handkerchiefs inside it.

The earlier generation, who played without the shoulder rest, wore suits made of heavier material. When they put the violin on their shoulder, with a handkerchief underneath, there was something more substantial to put the violin on. *So a pad inserted into the jacket is useful?* Some people have one put in. The shoulder rest is an extension of the pad, but further away—for me it is too inflexible.

* * * * *

Ruggiero Ricci doesn't like the shoulder rest. In his book on left hand technique he makes the humorous comment that the rot actually set in in an earlier period, when Spohr invented the chin rest! What he means is that, when the chin rest came in, it became easier to shift downwards. This process is taken further by the shoulder rest which, while adding security, can all too often lead to inflexibility in the left shoulder.

Vibrato

The first requirement for a fine vibrato is the desire to make a beautiful sound. Talented young players will often associate their ideal sound with that of a favourite virtuoso, whose tone quality has captured their imagination.

Vibrato must be rhythmic, not spasmodic. The most beautiful vibrato goes below the note and back up to it. When, in my early years, I used to play 78 records at half speed to observe the vibrato of the great players, I discovered that they all did it this way.

A vibrato that is both sympathetic and brilliant needs more horizontal movements of the finger, rather than just rotation.

This vibrato requires the finger to be put down square and go backwards quite firmly, to make the finger longer and get on to the pad. Then it comes back to the original square position.

Begin on the note, take the finger backwards, then firmly bump up to the pitch of the note. This is a movement in which you are going back and then firmly forward all the time, so that the top of the movement is the pitch of the note. The top of the movement uses the squarest part of the finger, which gives the brightest sound.

This exercise, in nine parts, gradually introduces the hand to this type of movement.

In exercises 2–9 the thumb remains in the third position.

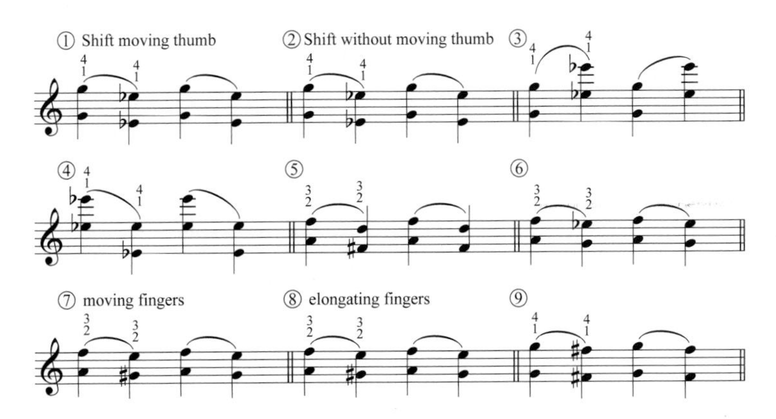

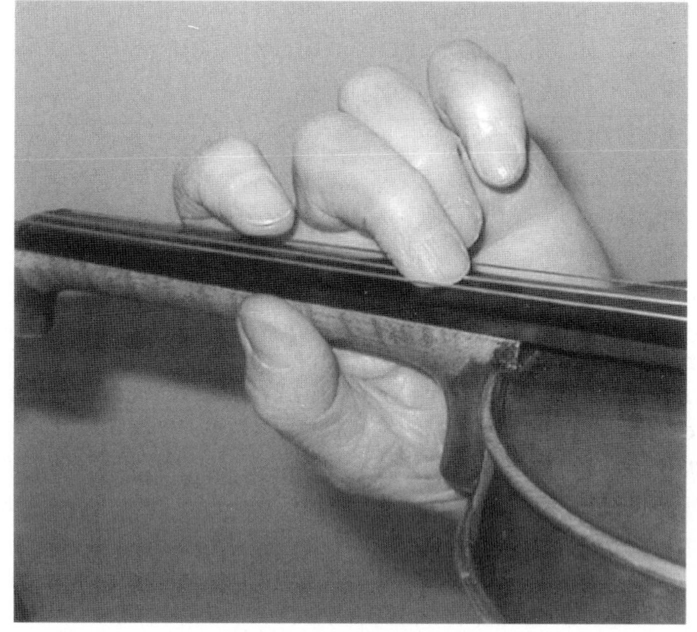

Michael Hurwitz

The forward position in vibrato

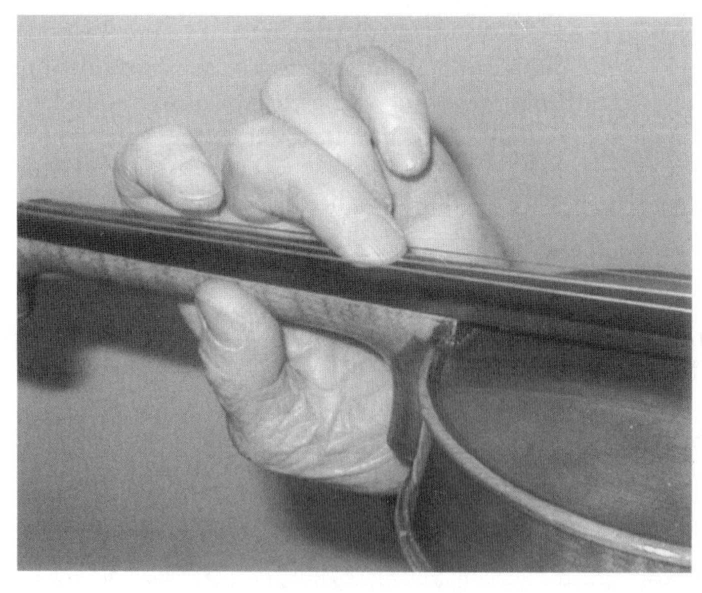

Michael Hurwitz

The backward position in vibrato

No.4, which swings a whole octave without moving the thumb, is a benevolent exaggeration, to find how free you can be while playing around the thumb.

Note the difference between No.7 and No.8. In No.7 the semitone is a shift: in No.8 the interval is made by elongating the fingers backwards—then moving forwards again.

After this, try rhythmic exercises going backwards and forwards on the finger without shifting.

First use a ♩♪♩♪ rhythm. Do this slowly, making sure that the weight is on top of the note, i.e. when the finger comes forward.

Then make even movements, gradually getting faster.

It is easier to learn this type of vibrato movement with two fingers down on two strings.

There is a contrary view, that is asserted by a few violinists, that vibrato should be on both sides of the note. Analysis carried out in America, about forty years ago, showed examples of vibratos going above the note. They all turned out to be singers who, unfortunately, often have this tendency.

Some players have a vibrato that sounds too stiff. They invariably have a restricted movement backwards and forwards, instead of the pull back followed by the forward movement.

Bleating is a vibrato that is like a trill, but without the finger leaving the string—an up and down movement. Players who bleat haven't got anything like enough backward movement in their fingers.

* * * * *

Playing is automatically more interesting if the fingers are put down in varying ways.

Playing on the pads will produce a more liquid and beautiful sound than playing on the fingertips.

Many violinists are unaware that they place their fingers far too squarely on the fingerboard.

It is very important to have good finger articulation.

In brilliant passages, generally the fingers need to be slightly squarer for clear articulation; for melodic playing they should be more on the pads.

In a slow movement, lift your fingers more gently.

If you put down a long finger, there's a difference in tone colour from when you put down a square finger. This is because the tip of

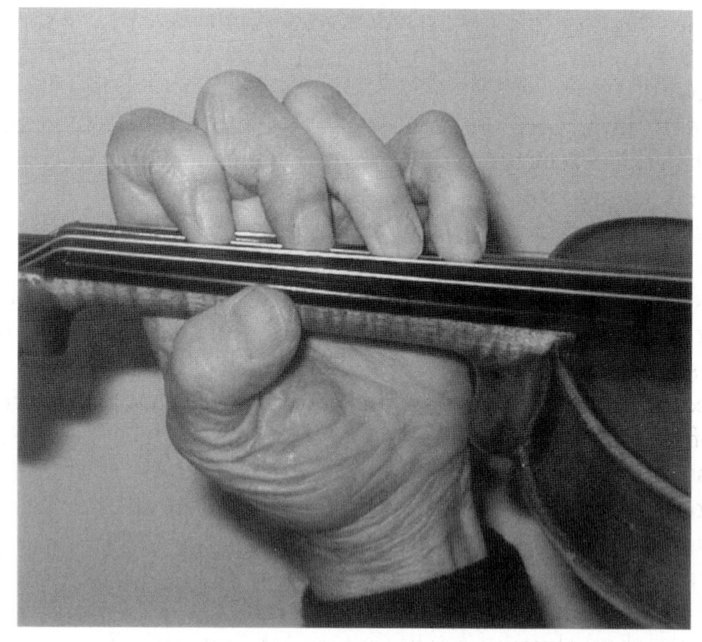

Michael Hurwitz

Wrong way—fingers on tips

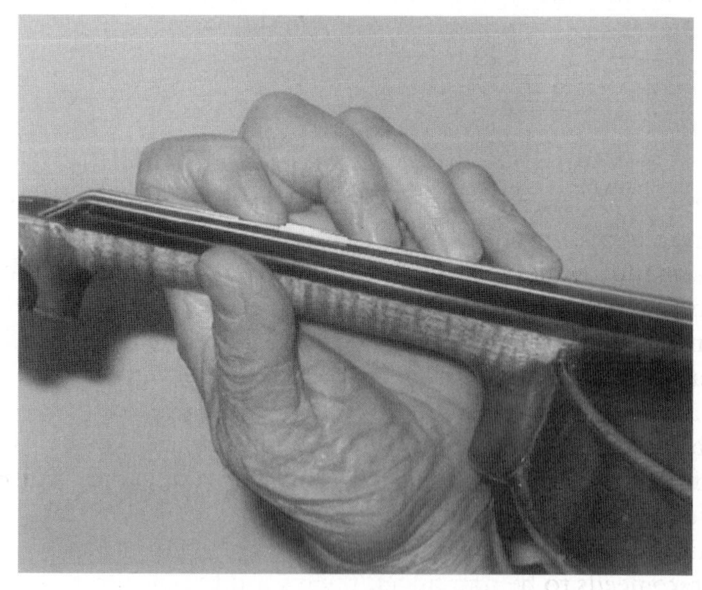

Michael Hurwitz

Right way—fingers sloping

the square finger is harder. The square finger produces a smaller vibrato.

When you put down a long finger, the contact with the flesh gives a different sound quality. A lot of interesting tone colouration comes from using different types of finger contact.

If I ask young violinists to play, with 1st and 2nd fingers, B and C sharp on the A string, followed by B and D, they generally put down their fingers in the same shape, using a different fingering, instead of just modifying the shape. The use of the half position and first position is very often a way of not having to make modifications of finger shape.

Maxim Jacobsen, in one of his idiosyncratic books, describes a way of massaging the string with your finger, to learn the different shapes of finger placement.

To be able to vary the vibrato, it is important to learn these different shapes. Many violinists play with their fingers in the same shape nearly all the time.

The fingers of the left hand should be independent of the thumb, which can then always be in the most comfortable place.

This is a good exercise for modifying the finger shape.

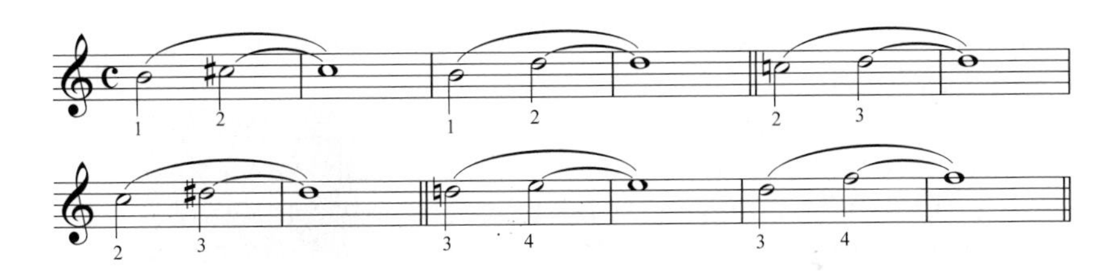

Keep the first finger down while commencing the second note so that, for a moment, both fingers vibrate. Then lift the first finger.

Most hands achieve the best control and most beautiful vibratos by using a combination of movements of the fingers, hands and arm.

Many players vibrate only in their hand and finger, which is too small a movement to make a really big sound. However, one should also learn to use a smallish vibrato, just having a feeling of energy in the fingertip, the hand and the whole arm—it is all alive.

Heifetz said that he felt his vibrato in his whole arm, right down into his fingers. By contrast, Kreisler said that he thought only of his fingertips.

Vibrato needs to be continuous from one note to another—it must not stop between notes.

If the vibrato is even, it is less intrusive. If it is varied, it gives a rich palette of colour, which most music needs, to a greater or lesser extent. This is very different from having just one automatic slip-on vibrato, which is musically uninteresting.

You shouldn't be extremely passionate all the time you are playing. Percival Hodgson said that nobody at the breakfast table says 'Pass the mustard' in a voice choked with emotion. Yet there are people who play with such a voice all the time!

It is important to vibrate more on the notes that are emphasised in the phrase, rather than equally on every note.

On the notes preceding an important note,you may not need so much vibrato. If those notes are too expressive there is nothing extra left for the important note. That's because it can't be emphasised in the same way, and then the high point of the phrase will be less interesting.

David Oistrakh, as a young man in his twenties, had a vibrato that was too fast. Later, he said that he had been trying to play like Heifetz. In his early to mid thirties he was fortunate in that his vibrato opened out naturally and became more opulent. Carl Flesch used to consider that it is not a problem if the vibrato of young virtuosi is small and fast because, as they get older, it tends to become slightly looser and slower. When Josef Hassid first heard his own recordings, he said that he was surprised how fast and unvaried his vibrato was. He wanted to modify this.

Many successful young players have got this virtuoso vibrato, which produces an intense warm sound of vitality and passion. It is true that the commercial world favours the exciting sound. However, there is a need to learn cooler sounds and shades of tone colour. This is particularly relevant in chamber music.

Szigeti speaks about the need for a leaner sound as a basic quality, so that then colour can be added or subtracted. By contrast Menuhin said that, when he was a boy of seven, his teacher would walk around him, hissing 'Vibrato, vibrato!'. Certainly a great vibrato should reflect the music, but in proportion to its contours.

Milstein, in a class, asked each student to start the slow movement of their concerto without any vibrato, to see how beautifully they could play with the left hand completely still. One of the students recalled that they found this nearly impossible, as they were all virtuoso trained!

Changing Position

The development of freedom of the left thumb is of great importance.

Allied to this is the need for elasticity in the left hand. Great players have both this elasticity and also freedom of the thumb, whether or not they use a shoulder rest.

If you do use a shoulder rest, practise for a few minutes each day without it. Then you can use the shoulder rest as a substitute for a pad, without the left shoulder becoming a solid block when holding the violin.

Exercises for left hand and thumb:

1 Play a semitone trill in third position, first with the usual 1 & 2 fingering, then with 1 & 3 and finally 1 & 4, getting the middle fingers out of the way. This is for maximum contraction of the hand.

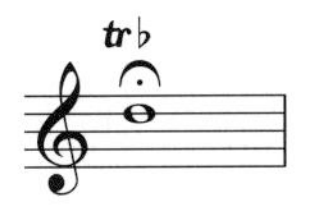

2 Alternating fingers:

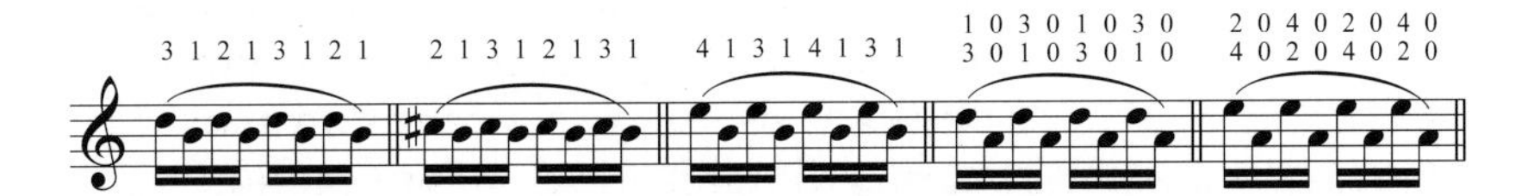

As the fingers alternate, the upper note should sound the same pitch. In the upper fingerings, the thumb is kept in the third position.

3 Exercise for different finger shapes:

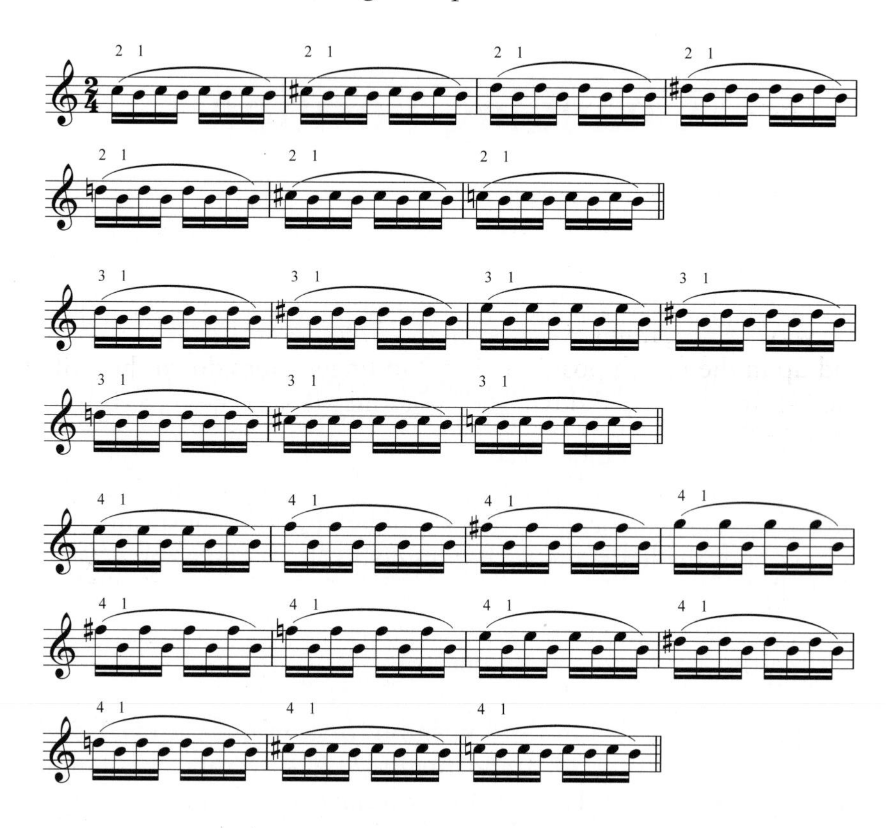

4 Repeat these exercises with the thumb in third position—this is an important variation.

5 Soft stretches, with or without the bow:

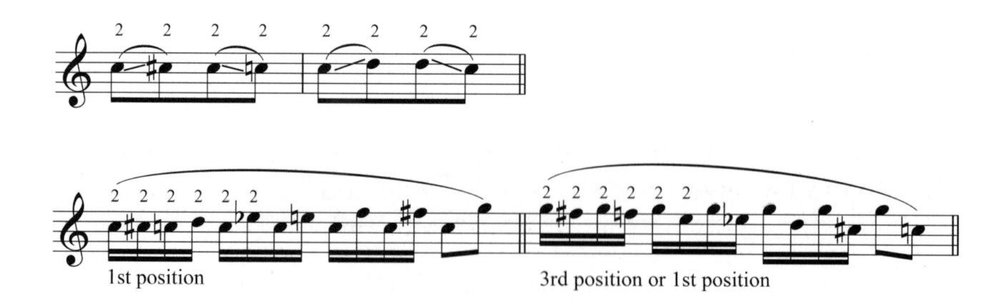

Then repeat the exercise, using the 1st, 3rd and 4th fingers.

6 Exercise for finger substitution:

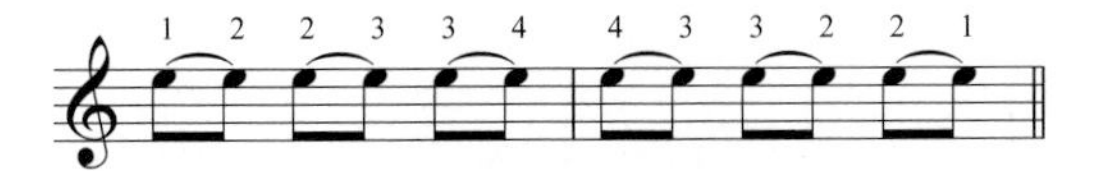

Here the flexible thumb moves just before the finger substitution. The hand starts in the fourth position and the thumb leads downwards when going to the 2nd finger, again for the 3rd and also for the fourth, so that the hand ends up in the first position. Then, on the way up, beginning 4 3, the thumb need not lead, but you should end up in the fourth position. The 2nd finger slides down the nail of the 1st finger, the 3rd down the 2nd, and the 4th down the 3rd (see page 132).

To make this possible, the 1st finger must be lengthened or flattened backwards, so as to make a soundless change of note. On the way up, the 3rd finger must squeeze as close as possible to the 4th, so as to have the smallest possible distance to cover at the moment of making the substitution.

The challenge is to make this substitution as inaudible as possible. It should be totally inaudible on the way down, and almost so on the way up. There should be a constant relaxed vibrato binding each pair of notes.

7 Repeat Ex. No.6, but without moving the thumb. This is a different way of using the left hand.

8 Arpeggio on one string:

For the 1st finger shift from B–F sharp: while playing the intervening D, advance the 1st finger to C sharp, lifting the 2nd finger out of the way.

When coming down, the 1st finger goes only as far as D, then the 3rd finger is substituted. This is the opposite approach to thinking in fixed positions.

Be prepared to move the thumb in advance of the hand, even when ascending the fingerboard.

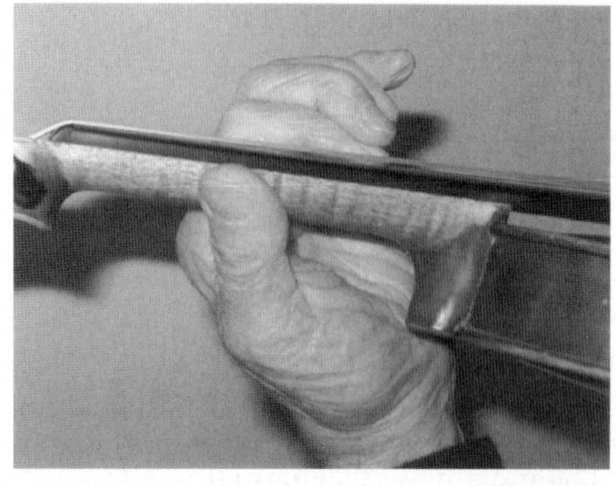

Michael Hurwitz

Second finger sliding down nail of first finger

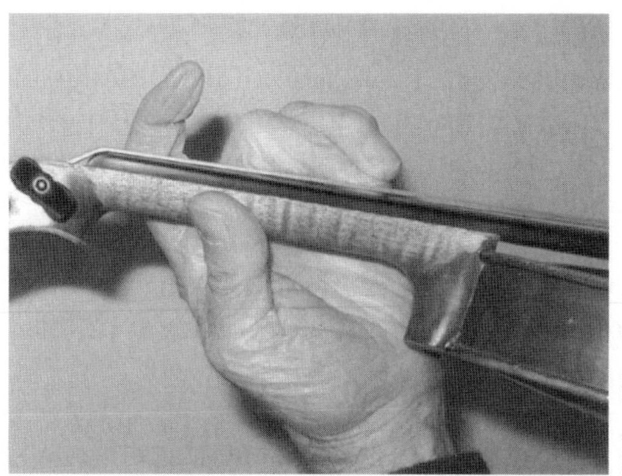

Michael Hurwitz

Third finger sliding down nail of second

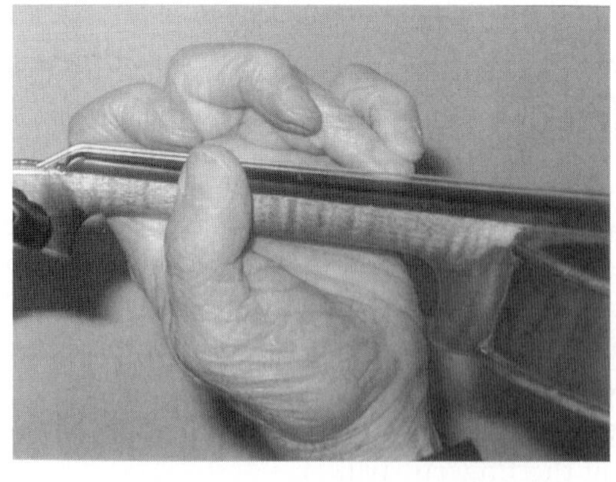

Michael Hurwitz

Fourth finger sliding down nail of third

9 The left thumb moving just before the shift is the pre-shoulder rest technique. Lack of independence of the left thumb can cause problems, even with advanced players.

Flesch called this system the expansion and contraction of the left hand.

Szigeti called it the 'langouste' (lobster).

Galamian called it the retarded shift. In his editions of solo Bach and other works, he uses a small circle around a fingering to indicate a stretch; and a square to indicate a shift in two parts—first the finger moves, then the hand.

Expansion and contraction are vitally important components of a free left hand. The great cellist, Feuermann, said that one should be able to play a scale so that a listener, who is not looking at you, cannot hear the sound of position changes or string crossings.

Just as the development of a fine vibrato is best done by working to an ideal held in the inner ear, seamless changes of position can be achieved by work at these exercises for flexibility, combined with careful listening.

10 Ysaÿe taught a scale exercise in which the 4th finger note was followed by the open string, in legato. This is for seamless string crossing.

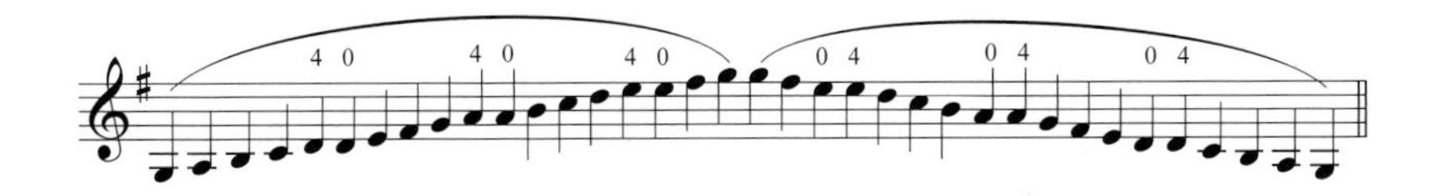

Ysaÿe would have expected the player to be accustomed to using open strings. Although nowadays it is unfashionable, it is useful to be able to play 3rd finger to open string on the way up, and open string to 3rd finger on the way down.

11 In Kreutzer No. 11, Carl Flesch introduced radically new fingerings, to encourage elasticity in the left hand. His edition included some explanatory notes on how to work at these studies.

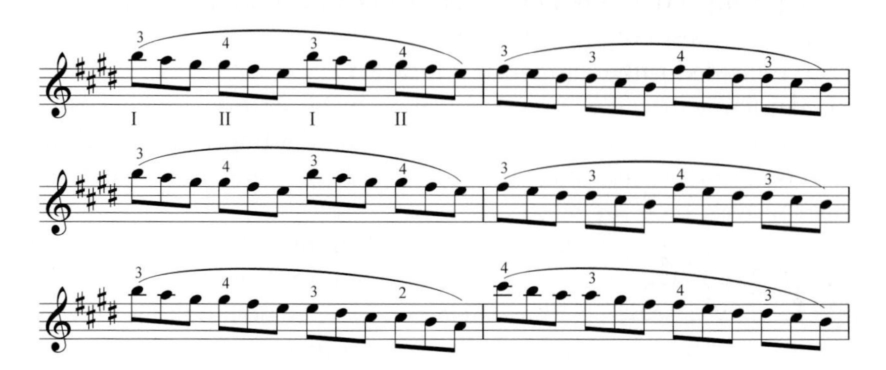

12 Play the six notes that form the second half of bar 2, repeating them several times without stopping.

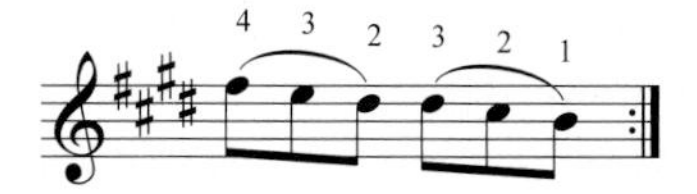

The thumb moves before the fingers, then the 3rd finger substitutes for the 2nd, sliding down the nail.

To reach the F sharp, the thumb advances to the second position, before the 4th finger stretches upwards.

Get used to advancing the thumb when shifting down; I also recommend first advancing the thumb when moving up. Thus, the shift is in two parts, with the hand following the finger, instead of moving simultaneously.

13 Two approaches to fingering this exercise, from different eras of violin playing:

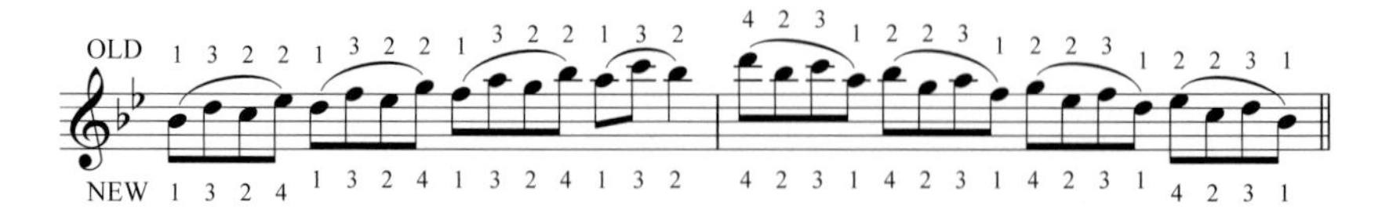

The old system used a 'guiding note' in which the 1st or 2nd finger shifts below the note to be reached. In the new system, the 1st or 2nd finger making the shift just goes as far as the note to be reached, before giving way to the finger that will play the note.

These are best considered to be alternative approaches. The only use of the 'new' fingering in print is in Rostal's edition of the Flesch Scale System.

14 A tenth in the first position:

In playing a broken tenth from the first position, advance the thumb to the third position, so that it becomes a natural extension, rather than a shift.

Practise octaves, using the 1st and 4th fingers, also with the 1st and 3rd. This gives a frame of reference for the left hand.

Expansion and contraction, if used inappropriately, can affect the intonation. At times it is necessary to jump, so as to create the right hand shape for the surrounding notes. Sometimes an extension can leave the hand out of shape. To avoid this it is preferable to jump.

The old style inclusion of an intervening note, to indicate how the finger shifts, gives a framework of reference that encourages good intonation. It is important to know this before learning the more sophisticated extension. Get used to practising both ways of shifting.

15

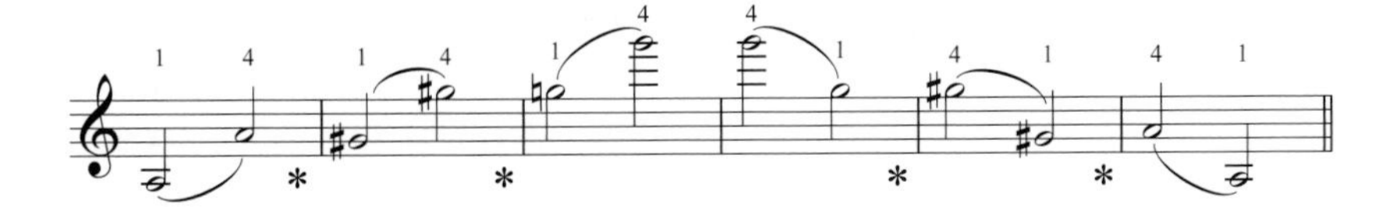

The stars indicate preparatory thumb movements. It is always important to consider the balance of the thumb. Try making experimental modifications of this exercise.

The same exercise in third position.

An exaggerated form of this exercise:

16 Rotate the thumb in fairly large circles on the neck of the violin, both clockwise and anticlockwise. The thumb should have the sensitivity of a dog's nose snuffling round a tree!

17 Herbert Whone, in his valuable book, **The Simplicity of Violin Playing**, gives an exercise: bow slowly in the air, just above the string, while raising and lowering the violin. Keep the bow at a constant height above the string, so that both arms are moving up and down together.

18 Carl Flesch gives a number of exercises for the flexibility of the left thumb in his small book **Urstudien** (Basic Studies). This book is intended for violinists who have only a limited time to practise. It is an invaluable collection of exercises.

19 For many young players, often the last thing that they learn is how to achieve security and freedom in the upper positions. The most successful way to achieve this is to swing the left arm around and slightly upwards, to keep the hand above the fingerboard. In this way you can be always in command at the top, instead of straining.

* * * * *

The movements that these finger exercises describe are those used by the lucky few who manage to find technical subtlety instinctively.

Bow Hold

There is a picture of Ernst, a mighty violinist, holding his bow in the first joint of the index finger. This bow hold is now obsolete but, in my early days, many people still played like that.

This was superseded by the Franco–Belgian bow hold, in which the bow is held between the first and second joints of the index finger, as taught by the school of Marsick, Massart, Ysaÿe, (via Wieniawski) and Capet, who taught Ivan Galamian in Paris.

Then came the Russian way of holding the bow: there are photos of the young Elman holding his bow above the second joint, dangling from the wrist. In the early years of the last century, the success of Elman, Heifetz and others from the Auer school, led to the belief that this was the right way to hold the bow.

In his autobiography Flesch said that, when writing his book on technique, he had to decide which was the best bow hold. Around 1890, when was a student at the Paris Conservatoire, the combined age of the four violin teachers was over three hundred. One of these, Dancla, was still holding his bow about four inches up the stick, in the old style. This is nearer the balance point and it is much easier to play in this way. In connection with this bow hold, Leopold Mozart, in 1760, said that a really fine violinist will bow past his own hand, thus using the whole bow.

There are some players who feel right with the Russian bow hold, while others prefer the Franco-Belgian way. It is just the way their body is built.

The video of Perlman and Zukerman playing duos is one of my favourites. Perlman holds the bow in the Russian style and Zukerman in the Franco-Belgian, yet they both studied with Galamian. Flesch always taught that extra bit of pronation of the Russian style, but two distinguished pupils of his, Ginette Neveu and Henryk Szeryng, didn't hold the bow in that way.

The Russian bow hold helps to glamorise the tone. I changed to it in 1944, after borrowing the Flesch books on technique. I found that it was a great bow hold, but I was worried that I was ruining my tone production, because it sounded so gritty. I probably didn't realise that I was getting to the centre of my sound—I just wasn't used to it.

When you begin a down bow, you need a sense of negative weight at the heel. As you progress towards the point, weight is gradually added by forearm rotation, known as pronation.

The reverse of this process is called supination, which is used as you approach the heel on the up bow. Flesch recommended a minimum of supination, whereas Rostal wanted more—in this they differed.

I overexaggerated Flesch's recommendation, which made my bow arm rather high. In the lower quarter, I didn't rotate the forearm and hand. I just kept my hand at the same angle, being unaware of the need for forearm rotation. I played like that until I started teaching seriously. Then I decided that I ought to look more normal, so that my pupils wouldn't be worried.

When I first discovered what it was like to rotate the forearm and hand at the heel, I preferred this approach. The problem of supporting the weight of the bow was removed. The act of changing the bow became much easier with this rotation.

In bowing, weight and movement have to be modified continually. Every bow stroke is a modification from a negative weight at the frog to perhaps half a pound at the point, going backwards and forwards.

The string is the opposition and the thumb is the fulcrum, bringing the whole forearm round with the arm swinging upwards.

If you are playing really strongly, you can hold the bow quite lightly. If you are playing softly, the bow needs to be held more firmly. Freedom, in the end, comes out of the entire arm, from the shoulder joint. Rostal said that if a teacher taps the wrist of the student, the bow should fall to the ground. It was easier to make experiments of this sort in my early days, when bows cost very little.

In bowing, there is the technique of the slow bow and the technique of the free bow.

But freedom doesn't mean a fast bow?

A very high proportion of players habitually use too fast a bow.

Fast, but not free, perhaps?

They think it's free, but it's just fast—which brings us to the subject of bow distribution.

Bow Distribution

Good bow distribution is a vital component in the art of playing the violin, or any stringed instrument.

Jacques Thibaud said that students always start off with a fast bow, whereas experienced artists enjoy sparing the bow.

At the heel, which is the heavy part of the bow, many players seem glad to get past the first few inches—they feel less comfortable there.

After a down bow, the up stroke from the point is usually too fast.

Would you agree that when there are four legato notes to play in one bow, very often the fourth note loses quality and volume? If you are running out of bow, the rhythm may get compressed, and the tone quality can deteriorate. Then the musical line suffers, because the phrase can become distorted through lack of sustaining power, particularly when making a crescendo on the down bow. Yes, this is something that I have taught quite passionately since I became aware of it as a young man. David Oistrakh, Szymon Goldberg and Max Rostal used to teach their pupils to give full value to the last note of a slurred group, allowing extra bow for it.

An absolutely vital exercise is to make sure that the fourth note has almost too much bow—so that the last note, at either end, has got a real connection with what follows.

Another exercise is to play a note of a given duration several times, beginning on a whole bow at medium speed, then gradually reducing the length of the stroke. You end up by using two inches of bow at the heel.

Then modify the exercise so as to end up at the point or the middle. Keep the same dynamic throughout.

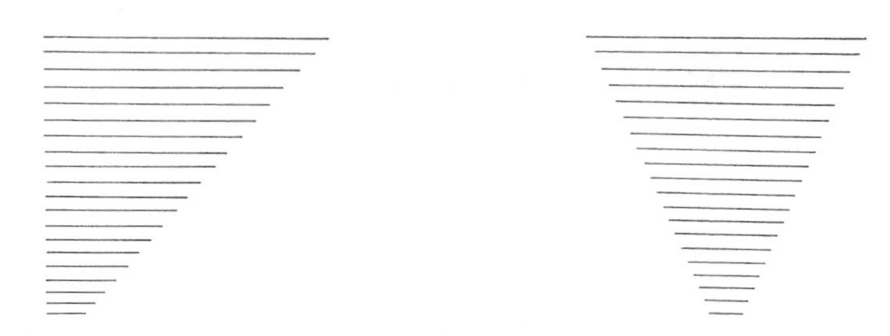

A fast bow tends to make the playing sound active and excited; a slow bow is much calmer and more placid in nature. Cultivate the feeling of a slower beginning to the bow stroke, with control.

In performance, if too much bow is used the playing may sound hysterical; with too little bow it can sound really boring and humdrum. Try this in solo Bach fast movements. A good player must learn to vary the speed and length of bow strokes.

I advise the practising of long slow bows, building up to thirty seconds or more. *It is said that Paganini could make a bow last for two minutes.* Yes, and that would have been on a bow about an inch shorter, with the hand held higher up the stick.

Players of an earlier generation, who used gut strings, could sustain a slow bow more easily than one can on the modern composite strings, on which the bow does not grip so easily.

A good exercise for bow distribution is to think of the down bow starting slowly, and increasing speed into the up bow, which also starts slowly.

The important book on bowing by Lucien Capet, one of the teachers of Ivan Galamian, has just been republished. Bow distribution exercises are rightly emphasised.

Bowing Exercises

1 Begin this exercise at the point. Use very little bow, but make the up bows slightly longer than the down bows. This causes you to shuffle down the bow.

As you move down the bow, adjust the balance of the arm, so as to feel comfortable doing this in any part of the bow.

Go right to the heel—which is a challenge.

2 This exercise is in the middle of the bow. Gradually lighten the down bows until you are only playing up bow quavers. The hand rotates from the wrist, with loose fingers.

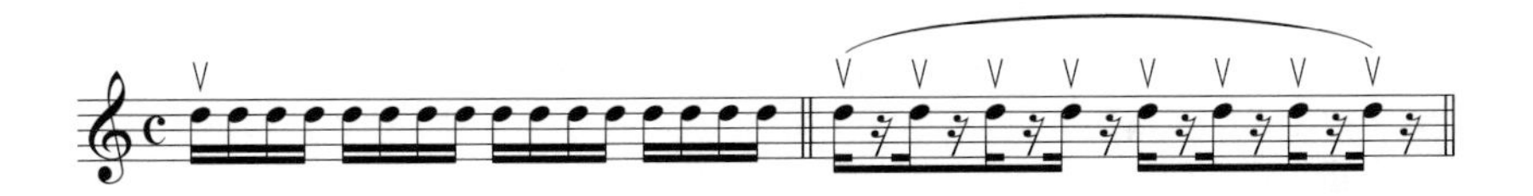

When this is mastered, try travelling along the bow at the same time. The following five examples show uses of this bowing.

In the last movement of the Mendelssohn Concerto, one has the choice of playing these quavers with a stiff arm, or with the freedom that the above exercise brings.

Adolf Busch used this bowing in Bach's Brandenburg Concerto No.4.

Schubert's String Quintet 1st mov. bar 118

The beginning of the 3rd mov. of the same work

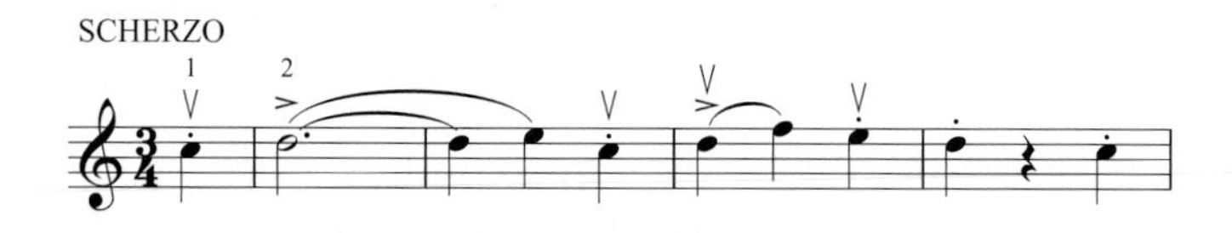

Bar 65 of the same Scherzo.

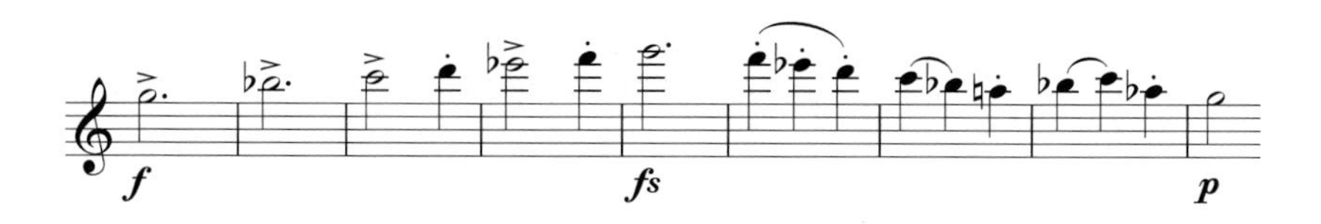

3 Play this rhythm with a slow shuffle down the bow.
Take about six shuffles to travel from the point to the heel.

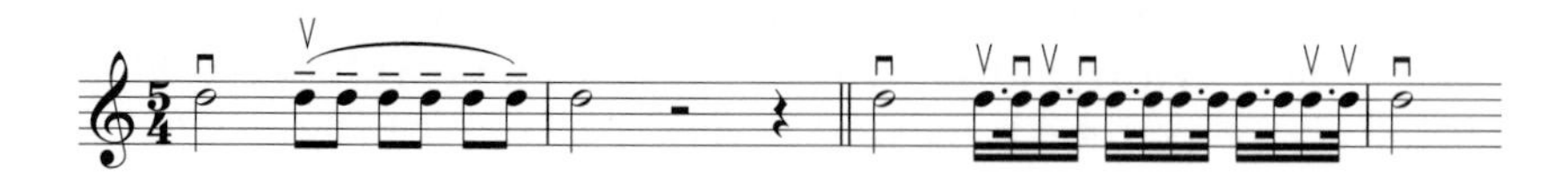

Then, on the down bow, repeat this, using longer down bows and shorter up bows.

In the first example, make the wrist higher on the longer up strokes and lower on the down strokes.

In the second example, only the short up stroke has the higher wrist.

4 Ysaÿe used an exercise in which the bowing arm is on seven levels, rather than the usual four.

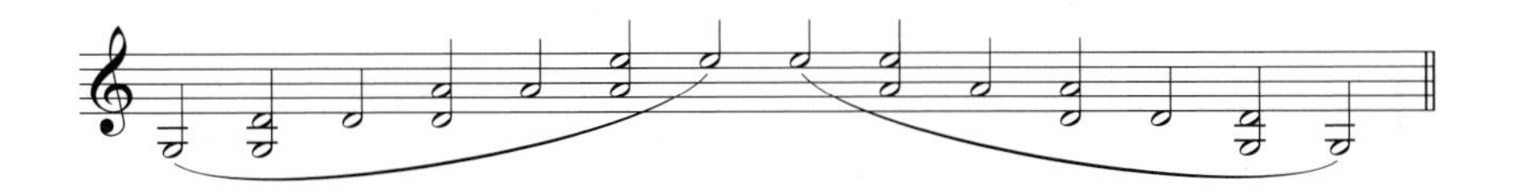

From this you can find a range of arm heights while playing on one string, moving the arm up and down without touching the adjacent strings.

5 This is an exercise that Rostal used to show pupils how to find a degree of flexibility in the wrist. Use open strings on the way up, the 4th finger on the way down.

One of the few points of technical information offered by Leopold Auer, in his short book on violin playing, is that freedom of the wrist is the most important element of bowing technique.

Both Flesch and Rolland said that you should leave the hand behind on the bow stroke in both directions.

Dounis said that the bow arm should feel slightly higher on the up bow than on the down bow.

6 A preparatory exercise for the previous example. Here the active wrist plays an important part.

7 This is an exercise that encourages a slightly swinging movement in the bow arm, to help create a smooth bow change. It begins in an exaggerated form on four strings, so that you can feel clearly the swinging movement.

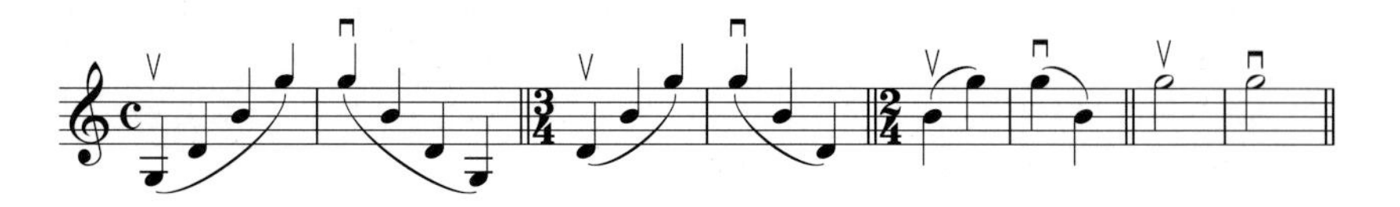

To learn this bowing, play a group of four slurred notes starting on an up bow. Then reduce the group to three, then two notes. Finally you are left with one note in the middle of the bow with a swinging action of the arm.

8 This exercise benefits from the slightly swinging motion of the previous example.

David Oistrakh taught this exercise for improving legato playing. By bringing the next note in early, one is encouraged to keep the bow moving. Gradually bring in the new note later and later, until you are not sure whether you have brought it in early or not.

Spiccato

Joachim used to describe to his pupils three basic types of spiccato: hail, rain and snow. Hail is the fast jagged one, rain the medium one, and snow is where you are just coming off the string at the end of the stroke.

The bow must never stop moving; the forearm is going gently backwards and forwards all the time.

I consider the technique of being able to play spiccato, with the up and down bows sounding the same as each other, as vital in rhythmic playing. Many violinists play the last page of the **Rondo Capriccioso** of Saint-Saëns too fast and, consequently, unclearly—with talent but without knowledge.

What would knowledge bring? Awareness of certain places where the string crossing will bring in the next note sooner, and other places where the string crossing will make it late. You have to know how to make these crossings work more evenly.

The way to do this is to understand the difference between the 'forward circle', used in the brilliant spiccato required in virtuoso music, and the 'backward circle' used in the longer spiccato usually associated with passages at a moderate speed in Mozart concertos or in chamber music.

It is essential to master both types. Many soloists are overreliant on the brilliant spiccato. Heifetz often speeds up passages in order to make his spiccato work more easily.

The brilliant spiccato

This is based on a forward or clockwise circle of the hand.

The first step is to understand this movement and to discover how it relates to string crossing.

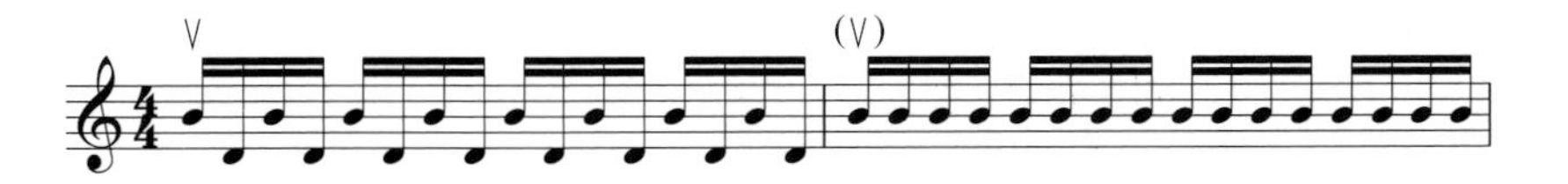

The next step is to continue this movement on one string.

The forward circle is the essence of the hand movement used in a brilliant spiccato. With this bowing, the down bow is the more dominant in sound.

The longer spiccato

This is based on the backward or anticlockwise circle—it is a longer movement.

Again, it is best learnt in relation to string crossing.

When using this movement on one string, it is like moving the hand inside a shallow bowl.

This spiccato is the one that gives control, especially for medium speed passages in Mozart and Haydn.

If you can do this, then you can make spiccatos of different height and length, which is incredibly important.

This backward circle is the one that promotes the rhythmic placing of semiquavers.

It is used in the beginning of the last movement of the first Schumann sonata, which is often played too fast and without control.

These circles imply a more musical attitude to bowing than the straight backward and forward movement. In the 1930s some photos were taken of Albert Sammons with a strobe light camera, which gave frequent shots of the movements made. The photography was done in the dark, with a small light on the end of his bow. All these photos show that there are no straight backward and forward movements. The natural movement of the arm from the shoulder doesn't produce this, so it is necessary to get rid of the concept of straight lines. These photos can be seen in a book by Percival Hodgson called **Motion Studies**, published by ASTA: it is one of the truly important books on technique.

There are videos from the 1960s of the great Hungarian teacher, Paul Rolland, teaching these movements. They show the wonderful freedom of technique that he taught to these young people. I consider that these short films are the best possible lesson for learning a stringed instrument. There are ten of them, still available from ESTA in Holland.

The person who didn't teach these movements was Suzuki. Originally, he based his exercises on a rather heavy martelé, straight backwards and forwards. The pupils I saw who used this method didn't play off the string. However, nowadays many Suzuki teachers have modified this approach. To play off the string with control and comfort is the basis for a good right arm technique.

Some players, who can play Paganini or Vieuxtemps concertos, have problems when they play a Mozart concerto, because the speed at which the semiquavers are played is just too slow to be played with the virtuoso's fast circle.

Another useful bow stroke is to imitate a slightly off the string bow at the heel, but playing it in the middle of bow. This is the bowing with holes in. I use it in the last movement of the Haydn Quartet Op. 76 No.6, which sounds too short and chopped up if played at the heel.

When playing this in the middle of the bow, the movement of the stroke is longer than the duration of the note.

A modification of an exercise used previously helps when learning this bowing. Play the group of four slurred notes near the middle of the bow, starting on an up bow.

Approach the string from the air, taking the bow off at the end of the stroke.

Then reduce the group to three, then two notes, gradually lessening the amount of bow used. Finally you are left with one note in the middle of the bow using a swinging action of the arm.

It's a bowing which Szigeti said was totally artificial but 'de luxe'—he called it 'floccato'.

Balance Between the Hands

The left hand and the bow are interdependent. With good tone production from the bow, one should be able to make a really good sound without using any vibrato. I ask my students to practise for a few minutes every day without vibrato. This greatly improves the subtlety of their tone production.

When you're dependent on vibrato, there is always the possibility that the bowing is not producing the best tone possible. I was taught by Pierre Fournier that you should be able to make a beautiful sound without using any vibrato. He spoke of then adding vibrato as 'the final colouring'. I agree, because you must have a balance between both sides of the body when you're playing.

You said that Huberman used very little vibrato in the slow movement of the Beethoven Concerto. To be able to do this would require a certain sophistication of bow technique. When I think about left hand and bow technique, I realise that they really are interdependent. Don't let the quality of your bowed sound be dependent on the vibrato.

The more you use vibrato, the less you might be using the right hand and right arm to the optimum degree. Adolf Busch often played with little, or only a small vibrato, but made a very big sound. *But do you think many violinists could do this?* It's not easy. One thing I'm very conscious of is that players tend to take more bows in certain passages these days than was the norm thirty or forty years ago. *How would you analyse this?* The bow works more easily when it's moving at a certain speed. To hold back and play with a very slow bow is a more difficult thing to do technically. A long, slow bow doesn't combine very successfully with a very small, fast vibrato. A player with such a vibrato tends to use a fast bow speed and plays more lightly.

If you look at any older edition of the Beethoven Concerto, you'll see that some passages in the slow movement have a whole bar in one bow.

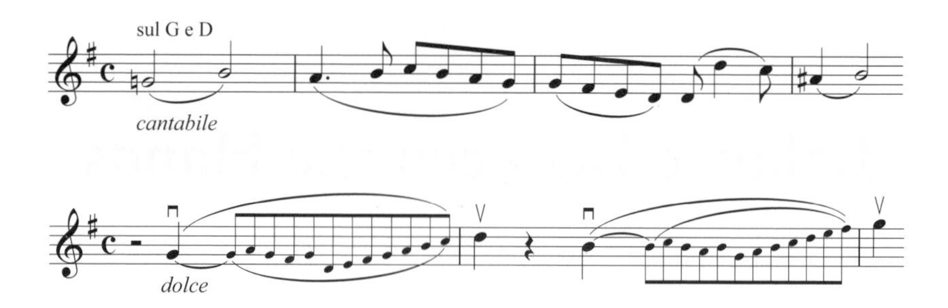

Today, you'll find that players, when the tune has two minims, will use a bow for each just to keep the bow travelling. If bowing in this way, you just haven't got the possibility of making the tune sound really slow.

Only a slow-moving bow gives the feeling of a musical passage moving gently. A faster bow gives a feeling that is less calm. When extra bows are taken there is not the possibility of the really 'clung' tone from the bow, a sound which gives that sense of tranquillity, essential in this Beethoven slow movement.

An important subtlety in legato is to be able to vary the intensity of the sound during the phrase. If the most important note of the phrase has got a little more bow movement than the one leading up to it, then the extra speed will give a subtle urgency to it: this can't be achieved in any other way.

The only person I remember teaching this was David Oistrakh. He taught pupils that an accent can be made by using a slightly longer bow on a note, in contrast to the jab accent. To achieve this it may be necessary to use less bow on certain notes and rather more on others. The first requirement for this is to cultivate the ability to travel with the bow at a constant speed. Many players can't do this because it needs very good bow distribution—perhaps the need for this accomplishment has not yet concerned them!

Great Violinists

Henryk Wieniawski

Introduction

Recently, on a long car journey, I listened to recordings of the ten Beethoven violin sonatas, played by Szigeti and Arrau. The second one that I put on was the Sonata in G, Op. 96. Later, after hearing all the others, I heard it for a second time and was utterly amazed to find that the playing sounded totally different—this time I liked it much more. Could there be a connection between this happening and the negative reactions sometimes expressed by students about great recordings of the past? These great performers played in a way fashionable to their time. They used more portamenti and rubati, which are alien to today's style. It can sound like a foreign language to modern ears.

You have heard most of the great violinists of the last century. For the rest of us, their playing can be heard on recordings, which now go back a hundred years—beginning with Joachim, who was born in 1831. They form a history of violin playing of the period, and show how styles and the various schools have evolved. I think that it is important for a teacher to direct students towards hearing great performances. Some quite famous teachers discourage their pupils from listening to works before they have studied them—so that they won't be influenced. I think that this is a totally wrong attitude. *They may have heard the piece many times before they begin with the teacher.* It's amazing how few concerts young people go to, often because they can't afford to. Although there is a multiplicity of recordings these days, there's a tendency not to listen to very many. Another danger is that one might buy the recording that just happens to be available in the shop. The greatest recordings tend to be from a long time ago; they usually cost much less than the latest ones.

If students hear something at a concert or on a recording that intrigues them, it will naturally influence their ideas about the piece. Ysaÿe said that he was inspired by hearing Wienawski play. Kreisler was influenced by hearing Ysaÿe. The young Menuhin would play along with Kreisler's recordings, just to feel what Kreisler's hands felt like and to study the portamenti and the different types of vibrato. The next day, he played with Heifetz's recording of the same piece. I did this myself in my early years.

By hearing these archetypal performances, students have something to measure themselves against. There have been only a few artists, on any instrument, whose playing feels just right musically. Don't just listen to one recording of a work—listen to two or three great players, to perceive a wider view of interpretative possibilities.

Students today have a further advantage: as well as recordings, they can watch various videos of great players. You can see how their technique is working, as there are close-ups that you won't have at a concert. A video which I've always encouraged my students to buy was made a number of years ago at the Royal College of Music by Izaak Perlman and Pinchas Zukerman, when they were both under thirty. They have an extraordinary energy. It is a wonderful example of two top-class violin talents really enjoying their playing. There's this feeling of collaboration, that they bring something together—they rub sparks off each other. Chamber music can have this wonderful build up, the subtlety is as rewarding, or even more so, than the impact of a concerto.

Prelude—Violinists of the Nineteenth Century

Before speaking of the great players that you have heard, let's begin with their most influential predecessors.

JOSEPH JOACHIM 1831–1907

What comments did you hear from musicians who had heard Joachim? They thought that at seventy (1901) he still had tremendous musical charisma. We can hear, in his two Bach recordings, that there's still a lot of virility left in his playing. These, and the two Brahms Hungarian Dances, show a violinist of great stature with a certain purity of style. Some of the shifts now sound rather scoopy, yet he was such an important artist that great singers, who didn't actually have to sound like that, would make portamenti like Joachim on the violin. *But is Joachim particularly associated with setting a style?* Very much so—he was a milestone amongst string players, right from the mid 1840s when he was a young boy. He first played the Beethoven Concerto in London at the age of thirteen.

My teacher, Sydney Robjohns, studied with him on summer courses in Germany in the 1890s. He thought of Joachim as a giant musician: nothing was played without meaning. There was nobility of phrasing, rhythmic brilliance and magical contrasts: melodies played with a seemingly endless bow; the only player he thought equal to Joachim in this was Ysaÿe.

A book called **Studying with Joachim and his Quartet in Germany**, written anonymously, mentions several precepts that Joachim demanded. I realised that my teacher had passed these ideas on to me. One of these was the serious study of bow division. Most players, after a down bow, start the up bow a little faster than they should. I was told to practise counting one, two, three, four on the

Joseph Joachim

whole bow, and then to use just a quarter of the up bow on the next crochet. Joachim taught his pupils to use the bow at the heel—to practise using the last two or three inches of the up bow, because no one's going to be comfortable until they play there long enough to find it friendly. I was told to use plenty of rosin at the heel, to get a good martelé bite.

Joachim said that there are two ways of starting a bow stroke. One is by putting the bow on the string before starting the note, the other one is starting with a moving bow, and coaxing it into the string. That is the one that isn't used enough. If a bow has more than one slurred group of two notes, when phrasing off each second note you must have a flexion. The bow doesn't stop at all—everything must be free.

Joachim hated a big slow vibrato. He said it sounds like the wailing of old women! You can hear that occasionally he used a close vibrato.

I knew an elderly pianist who heard him play Brahms, at the turn of the century. He said it was mighty music making, of great grandeur. Szigeti said that, in his own recording of the Brahms D minor Sonata, he's really doing the Joachim tempi, some of which were slower than are usually played today.

The musical stature of Joachim is well illustrated by the wonderful cadenzas he wrote for the Beethoven and Brahms concertos, also for the fourth and fifth of Mozart. His own concerto is full of exceptional virtuoso difficulties: it is interesting, but not first rate. There is a fine recording of it by Aaron Rosand.

PABLO DE SARASATE 1844–1908

Sarasate represented the opposite polarity to Joachim. He was both virtuoso and a fine composer for his instrument. He was the first player that my father heard after his arrival in Europe in 1907. When I asked him about it, he just remembered an old man who played very fast. I still have the programme of the concert. Carl Flesch said that Sarasate taught us to play in tune. Sarasate's recording of his own

Pablo de Sarasate

SALLE DE LA GRANDE HARMONIE

Mercredi 27 Novembre 1907, à 8 1/2 heures du soir

GRAND CONCERT

donné par

PABLO DE SARASATE

VIOLONISTE

ET

Berthe Marx-Goldschmidt

PIANISTE

PROGRAMME

Troisième sonate pour piano et violon, en *ré* majeur . .	MOZART.
Allegro con spirito; Andante cantabile; Allegretto, Allegro.	
Mme Berthe Marx-Goldscmidt et M. de Sarasate.	
a/ Ouverture de la vingt-neuvième cantate . . .	BACH.
b/ Etude de pédalier	SCHUMANN.
c/ Etude en forme de valse	SAINT-SAËNS.
Mme Berthe Marx-Goldschmidt.	
a/ Chaconne, b/ Largo, c/ Allegro assai } des sonates pour violon-solo . .	BACH.
M. Pablo de Sarasate.	
a/ Carnaval mignon, op. 48	EDWARD SCHÜTT.
Préambule — Sérénade d'Arlequin — Tristesse de Colombine Polichinelle — Pierrot rêveur — Caprice Sganarelle	
b/ Rapsodie hongroise, nº 10	LISZT.
Mme Berthe Marx-Goldschmidt.	
a/ Chansons russes pour violon.	SARASATE.
b/ Danse espagnole nouvelle, op. 52 : *Iota de Pablo* .	SARASATE.
M. Pablo de Sarasate.	

Molto de l'op. 52 : « Dans l'exquise fraîcheur de l'Aube le Rythme aimé, joyeux, qui la nuit montait aux étoiles, s'éloigne lentement... et reste dans le Rêve. »

Accompagnateur : OTTO GOLDSCHMIDT

PIANO ÉRARD

PRIX DES PLACES : Place numérotée (1 à 208), **6** fr. ; Place numérotée (209 à 340), **4** fr. ; Premier banc de la Galerie, **6** fr. ; Galerie, **2** fr.

S'adresser chez **MM. BREITKOPF & HÆRTEL,** 45, Montagne de la Cour

Impr. Th. Lombaerts, Mont. des Aveugles, 7.

Programme of a Sarasate concert of 1907

Introduction and Tarantella came out at the same time as his E major Preludio of Bach. His own piece is superbly played. He's using a gut E string, which makes the fifths more difficult. It has speed and flair, but his performance of the Bach is really very careless. *He may have speeded it up to get it on to one side of a record.* The tempo wasn't any faster than that of his own Tarantella, which is more difficult.

There is a story about Sarasate meeting Ysaÿe at a concert where Joachim played the Brahms Concerto. Sarasate said that he did not want to perform a work in which the only good tune is played by the oboe. In the 1880s, Joachim was welcome anywhere, so long as he didn't play the Brahms Concerto—a work that at first was not popular. A critic called it a concerto against the violin!

EUGÈNE YSAŸE 1858–1931

Eugène Ysaÿe was a fascinating link between the past and the present. I remember Ernest Read telling me how, quite by chance, he had heard Ysaÿe play the Beethoven Concerto. Not being a violinist, he had come to the concert because of other works in the programme. He was amazed how wonderful it was.

Eugène Ysaÿe

On Ysaÿe's recordings you can hear phenomenal ability. At times he does old style portamenti. Often he uses a very intense and beautiful vibrato, which belongs to the modern period. Sometimes I find that his vibrato is a bit fast and a little too tight, something common to many violinists.

In those days, no one would have dreamt of practising to achieve the perfection that later became the norm. Ysaÿe sometimes took risks. His Mendelssohn Finale really is a gallop, probably to get it on one side of a record. It ends up with the pianist being left behind; also the speed affected the intonation. Szigeti said that Ysaÿe sometimes used strange fingerings that were very risky. He'd plunge his fourth finger out, perhaps up a fifth on the G string. One night he would reach it and another night he wouldn't. It didn't matter so much in those days—people weren't so worried about technical perfection.

Fritz Kreisler said that he couldn't imagine how he would have played if he hadn't heard Ysaÿe. *Did Joachim like Ysaÿe's playing?* I think he liked it very much, but it was very different from his. Ysaÿe asked him to come to hear him play the Brahms Concerto. When asked afterwards for comments, Joachim said that he had played it wonderfully, but that it was so idiosyncratic that he ought to call it the Brahms–Ysaÿe Concerto.

Klingeler, whose daughter founded the music competition in Munich, was very talented as a boy and had had the choice of going to study either with Joachim or Ysaÿe. His daughter remembered her father saying 'So I chose to go to the great musician'. Ysaÿe, to him, was merely a great virtuoso. Opinions were divided at the turn of the century—those in the Joachim camp thought Ysaÿe was just a temperamental virtuoso; those in the Ysaÿe camp thought that Joachim was rather exact and pedantic. My teacher was from the Joachim side.

Ysaÿe recorded twelve pieces at a session in 1914, when he was a little past his prime. Nevertheless, they give evidence of his collosal talent.

Violinists that I Heard and Worked with

FRITZ KREISLER 1875–1962

Kreisler began his career as a prodigy, winning first prize at the Paris Conservatoire at twelve, after which he received no further violin tuition—he advised other players not to take lessons beyond fourteen. Two years later he toured in the USA. For a while he studied medicine, and he also considered a career as an army officer, in which capacity he later served, for a short time, in the Austrian army at the outbreak of the war in 1914.

Kreisler made many recordings, starting around 1915. His concertos of Beethoven, Mendelssohn and Brahms, recorded in Berlin from 1926–7, are very fine—preferable to the second recordings of those works that he made in London from 1935–6. Also remarkable are the recordings of his own compositions.

There is an account of the meeting of Joachim and Kreisler that clearly shows how different they were. Joachim attended Kreisler's debut in Berlin in 1905. The following morning, Kreisler came to listen to Joachim's master class. The pianist didn't turn up so Kreisler immediately stepped in, playing all the accompaniments from memory. At the end of the session, he was introduced to Joachim whose only comment was 'You are indeed an able pianist'. Joachim probably felt that Kreisler inhabited a different world to him. It would have been so much outside his terms of artistic reference that he couldn't take it totally seriously.

Carl Flesch first heard Kreisler play in 1905, the year of his debut in Berlin. He said that at that time people were a little embarrassed by the sensuality of his playing. They could hear that he was tremendously talented, but considered that his sound really belonged to hotel and light music playing. *Perhaps that's the reason why it took him a while to gain universal acceptance.* Yet, after he became world

Fritz Kreisler

famous, his unique sound made a number of other players seem out of date, and their careers declined accordingly. *It was rather like that with Casals on the cello.* The records I've heard of Casals' contemporaries, like Becker and the leader of the Berlin cellos, sound very old-fashioned in their shifting.

When did you first hear Kreisler? I was very fortunate to hear him when I was a small boy. My parents used to take me to his recitals, usually at the Queen's Hall. I remember that Kreisler's concerts were always sold out.

What are your memories of hearing him? I remember how he would stroll on to the platform, very amiably and comfortably. Harold Schonberg, in the New York Times said that, whereas Heifetz looked like a champion about to defend his title, Kreisler looked as if he were coming to play to his friends. There was a warmth of personality and a total absence of any pretentious gestures. Everybody felt that he was playing just for them. He made such a beautiful sound that I very passionately wanted to develop a tone like his. It was magic to experience live what I had come to love and be excited by on his records. Directly you heard him play you realised that, apart from this wonderful sound, there was the most inimitable phrasing.

Was Kreisler a very expansive personality on the platform? He was fairly restrained, and didn't move about that much, rather like Milstein and Heifetz, who were self-contained dynamos of energy. Their machines were working so marvellously that there didn't need to be any extra movement.

Did you play with him? Just in one concert. It was one of those Sunday afternoon concerts of the LPO. I forget who was conducting those shows, but it could easily have been Beecham. Kreisler played the Mendelssohn and the Tchaikovsky. I remember him handing out a whole lot of manuscript paper to the orchestra, to put in his own composed ending to the slow movement of the Tchaikovsky. Normally the slow movement just melts into the start of the last movement, but he said he'd like to have a rest and a tune before playing the last movement, so he played his own version of these last few bars.

How did playing with him compare with hearing him from the audience? When you're playing with a person who is an absolute legend, there is a tendency to try to listen as much as possible and not play your own part all that wonderfully. I was sitting on the outside of the first violins, not too far away from him. *Was he easy to accompany?* Oh yes, very easy; everything was tremendously logical.

Joseph Gingold, when he was leading one of the major symphony orchestras, said that Kreisler came to play the Brahms Concerto. They got on very well and, after the concert, Kreisler said 'Come with me tomorrow night; I'm doing a recital about forty miles away. The next night he travelled out with Kreisler and they had a good early dinner at about half past six, with a little wine. Literally half an hour before the concert Kreisler said 'Well, I'd better change and go to the hall'. He started the concert with the Spring Sonata, and Gingold realised that he was just using this to play himself in: he was not too concerned about it. When he got into his stride, he played absolutely wonderfully. Kreisler said 'I really don't like knowing things too well, because it takes away from the adventure and the thrill of the concert'.

One quite often hears young violinists playing some Kreisler pieces in their recitals, but you can tell that they haven't really studied the way that Kreisler played them—they're just too strait-laced. I remember an article by Szigeti in the 1950s, talking about the magic of Kreisler's playing of his own pieces; how you hear certain passages being pulled back and others moving on, in a way that brings life to the music. However, the critics used to complain that, although Kreisler played wonderfully, he played too many short pieces in his recitals and not enough major works.

The Auer School

MISCHA ELMAN 1891–1967

Around 1915, before the appearance of Heifetz, Mischa Elman was considered more or less the world's number one violinist. There was a straight line from Ysaÿe to Kreisler and then to Elman.

I first heard him, playing the Tchaikovsky Concerto, when I was thirteen. The tone production was not more beautiful than Kreisler, but more sensuous. His phrasing was very spacious, but I felt he was pulling the music around more than other players—he had a very elastic approach to rubato. He would often stretch out a note much longer than the conductor expected.

I met him several times through my friend Felix Vandyl. On one occasion he showed us a couple of press cuttings from one of his concerts. One critic said he was wonderful, the other that he used far too much rubato. Elman said 'I go my own way!'

I played viola in a quartet with him at a friend's house one night, with Christopher Bunting on cello and Raymond Cohen playing second violin. When we arrived, we found that our wealthy Hampstead host had put out about twenty chairs for all his friends to listen. We were about to play the Dissonance Quartet of Mozart. The old Peters Edition has, after the exposition, an awkward page turn. Elman said 'I've got a nasty turn here. Is there someone who can turn over for me—anybody who can read music'. A voice from the front said 'A little'; it was Max Rostal. Afterwards they were introduced to each other.

Sometimes Elman brought a string quartet to his recitals, playing the **Cantabile** of Tchaikovsky, and the slow movement of Dvorak's **American Quartet**, or the second Borodin. The New York Times critic, Harold Schonberg, a very witty man, said that Elman used his three colleagues in the string quartet like an acrobat uses a safety net!

I heard him play both in concerto and sonata performances, also

Mischa Elman

in concertos with piano. In the 1920s and '30s it was very fashionable to play the Mendelssohn, Wieniawski or Bruch Concerto with piano accompaniment as part of a recital. That has now gone out, which is a pity, because if you hear one of the concertos with piano, you're liable to hear a lot more of the details of the solo part than you do when they're playing with orchestra.

His hand was very plump, with not particularly long fingers. His sound was wonderful, although not quite so much so after the age of fifty. *I first heard him in 1961, playing the Mendelssohn and Brahms concertos. He tended to avoid having to play fast by initially moving forward, almost getting ahead of the orchestra, so that he then could take more time over the fast passage. I also remember him joining in a section of the opening ritornello of the Brahms so as to warm up. Later, I heard him in two recitals with piano, also at the RFH. In one he included the Wieniawski D minor Concerto, and in the other the Mendelssohn. He still had an extraordinarily beautiful way of handling the instrument.*

JASCHA HEIFETZ 1901–1987

Did you hear Jascha Heifetz in the earlier days? I heard him give several recitals, back in the 1930s, in the Queen's Hall. When I heard him play Vieuxtemps, Wieniawski or any of the virtuoso pieces, it was a different world of violin playing to the one that I inhabited. He was a most exciting player. There was a sense of risk-taking and dare-devilry, demonstrating the triumph of technical difficulties overcome.

Heifetz was the virtuoso to whom every other violinist deferred, with the possible exception of Milstein. Listening to all the great post-war virtuosi, I don't think that anyone matched his sheer talent for playing everything with such comfort, elegance and ease. Over the last twenty years, I've heard a number of young violinists with a phenomenal talent similar to that of Heifetz. Yet if you listen to a recording of a virtuoso work by any of them and then put on the Heifetz version, you may notice that his imagination and range of tone colour is incomparable. The mercurial rubatos were so personal, characteristic and charismatic. However, some students nowadays prefer certain contemporary players.

The first time I worked with him was when he recorded the **Symphonie Espagnole**. I was playing as an extra in the Philharmonia Orchestra. That record only came out recently, having been made in the 1950s.

Quite often I felt that he was doing things which were really risky, but they always came off. The last time I heard a recital of his was at the Festival Hall, in the late '50s. In 1962 I heard him record in London Vieuxtemps No. 5 and Bruch's **Scottish Fantasy**. I went there for a couple of days. He was still at the height of his powers; it was playing of unparalleled virtuosity. *I was also there for that amazing Bruch recording and always remember it.*

Two or three recordings never came out. One was the Kreutzer Sonata with Rubinstein, which he didn't let out because he thought there was too much piano. They recorded it again later, with a little less piano sound. To a virtuoso, it doesn't matter how important the piano part is—it's always an accompaniment.

There were two of his early records that I listened to over and over again, when I was nine or ten. One is the **Scherzo Tarantelle** of Wieniawski and the other was **La Ronde des Lutins** by Bazzini. Heifetz is definitely employing some of the earlier styles of shifting in these pieces. *But without that groany quality that some players had in their shifts.* In the Bazzini, although beautifully smooth, there

Jasha Heifetz
(Courtesy Norman Rosenberg)

is sometimes a more leisurely connection between notes. It's not yet vintage Heifetz, but it's incredible violin playing. Later, he employed the gypsy way of shifting on the finger you are going to. It became something of a mannerism in the 1950s.

To me, Heifetz was at his greatest in less important music. As a young man, when I heard him play the Mozart, Beethoven, Mendelssohn and Brahms concertos I didn't find them as satisfying as when played by Kreisler or Szigeti. *But Heifetz had a mercurial quality that gave a different dimension to technique?* Absolutely, there was always this control which would allow rubato or shaping—it was never mechanical.

The way he held his violin and bow was very personal. Virtuoso violinists of his generation held the violin on the shoulder and fairly high. On the bow, he had his first finger so much around the stick that, when he was about forty-five, he was becoming very uncomfortable in the lower part of the bow. He went to have some lessons from Demetrius Dounis, a great teacher of the time. Dounis said 'Well, seeing it's you, I can't call them lessons—we'll call them consultations'.

I remember that I held my bow this way—from the time I read the Flesch book. I practised playing in the top half of the bow with only the first finger on the stick. At that time most of my younger friends were having lessons with Rostal. He was teaching them to drop the elbow slightly, when they came past the middle to the nut, with the forearm and hand slightly rotating towards the third and fourth fingers. This was totally correct. At the time I thought that it was really rather cissy to do a thing like that, because the Carl Flesch approach was to go remorselessly backwards and forwards, just balancing on the little finger.

So Rostal was different from Flesch in that way? Rostal, Goldberg and Szeryng all had a tendency to hold their bows with the first finger not quite so passionately advanced. I saw in a magazine a picture of various players bowing. Ginette Neveu, a Flesch pupil, was definitely holding her bow just in front of the second knuckle, instead of having it dug right in.

In that marvellous video of Perlman and Zuckerman playing duos, these two young men are holding their bows quite differently from each other, and they are both working wonderfully. Perlman plays holding it the Heifetz way—the way he'd been taught in Israel, before he came to America. Zuckerman changed to holding it in the lever fulcrum way, the Galamian approach. Although Flesch taught a bow hold similar to that of Heifetz, most of his great pupils didn't hold the bow as far up the index finger as that.

I tell pupils that if a teacher says that theirs is the only possible way of playing, leave immediately.

NATHAN MILSTEIN 1904–1992

I remember the first time I heard Milstein was in a Sunday afternoon concert, I think in Covent Garden, in 1935. He was a giant of a player, always electrifying although, for me, there wasn't the magic personal touch of my heroes.

Nathan Milstein
(Courtesy Tully Potter Collection)

One thought of Milstein as a virtuoso of a similar calibre to Heifetz, although his musical desires were certainly not to be flamboyant, but to be cool and classical. He would often, on purpose, play a traditionally expressive passage with restrained emotion, while choosing an unexpected place to do something wonderful. His appeal lay in the purity and ease of his technique.

I heard him play the Tchaikovsky just after the war in the Haringey Arena, which was a dog racing track: it was a very large enclosed building, rather like the Albert Hall. I distinctly remember finding that the strings of the orchestra sounded a bit vague and woolly, both in the overture and in the opening of the Concerto. However, when Milstein came in, I heard him perfectly, although I was sitting very far back. He never went for an enormous sound, but its sheer quality and focus was very impressive.

His old recordings of Mozart concertos are wonderfully eloquent, if not very deep. Also very fine are his recordings of the Tchaikovsky and Goldmark concertos and the solo Bach works. While he was recording the Goldmark, Hugh Bean said that if one had to show someone from another planet what a pure violin sound could be like, this would be the one to choose. *In 1965 I heard him give an extraordinary performance of Bach's C major fugue at the RFH. The intonation was so pure that the sound completely filled the hall.*

Would you say that his and Heifetz's were the two greatest techniques? Well let's say they were two of the greatest techniques of the time. Neither of them played as mercilessly correctly as Leonid Kogan, who played some of the virtuoso pieces like a computer.

How much do you feel that the particular school that a great player has come from influences their approach to sound production? It is in the basic approach to sound production that players differ. *But isn't that where a particular school does show?* I think that it's more individual. I don't think that any of the greatest players had to learn vibrato. They were blessed with something that worked marvellously for them. There are a lot of players with great virtuosity in their machinery who don't possess this beauty of sound.

I had the good fortune to play quartets with Milstein in the 1960s, at the home of an outstanding amateur cellist, Dr. Edward May. Manoug Parikian played second violin and I played viola.

OSCAR SHUMSKY 1917–2000

Shumsky was one of the last Auer pupils. For some reason his solo career was largely made in his sixties. As a young man he had great success as leader of the Primrose String Quartet and he was a highly regarded teacher. I heard his first concert in London: this spectacular recital was entirely for solo violin. It included a fiendishly difficult fugue by Reger and, after playing the third Partita by Bach, he played the second Ysaÿe sonata, which begins with quotations from that work. The encore, Kreisler's **Recitative and Scherzo**, he made seem a big piece of music.

He made a wonderful sound, but it was perhaps a little too controlled. On other occasions I heard him play the Concerto No. 1 of Saint-Saëns, which showed tremendous virtuosity, but the Tchaikovsky Concerto sounded routine and not particularly interesting. *I heard him give a wonderful performance of Spohr's* ***Gesangescenen Concerto****: it was immaculate playing.*

My Other Major Influences

To me, there were four great violinists with tremendous musical personalities. We have already spoken of Kreisler; the others were Szigeti, Huberman and Busch.

JOSEPH SZIGETI 1892–1973

What were your impressions of Szigeti in concert? Szigeti played everything with marvellous musicality. I was much attracted to his phrasing for its subtlety and his shaping of melodies, which always seemed correct. His playing sounded aristocratic and it had a wonderful rhythmic drive.

I found it interesting that a player who didn't have the wonderful left hand sound of Kreisler or Heifetz could play with such eloquence. I realised that it was largely due to his magnificent bow technique. He could draw the bow extremely slowly, getting a wonderful legato sound. He also had a mastery of short bowings and different types of staccato.

Although he was a fine virtuoso in his own way, his technique was considered by Carl Flesch to be obsolete; particularly his bow technique—Flesch wrote that it should have been consigned to the rubbish heap long ago. There is no doubt that he was not naturally built to play the violin. He was tall and gangly, with long arms and fingers—it wasn't the smoothest machine functioning—yet, somehow, he made his technique work for great music. Certain recordings are the equal of any—his Mozart in D, Beethoven, Mendelssohn and Brahms concertos and his Prokofiev No. 1—these are wonderful performances.

When I first heard Szigeti, playing the Brahms Concerto, I was in the third or fourth row of the Queen's Hall—quite near him. Initially I was disappointed that there wasn't more sound. A recording can have a very artificial balance. *But didn't the Queen's Hall have a very*

Joseph Szigeti
(Courtesy Tully Potter Collection)

good acoustic? A very good acoustic yes, but I was sixteen, and was comparing it with his recording.

In the 1930s, only Szigeti and Kreisler had recorded the Brahms Concerto. I knew these records so well. *Did you hear Szigeti play the Brahms before Kreisler?* Yes. Because it was the first recording I'd heard of this piece, it seemed the right way to play it. Often, the first way you hear something has a tendency to be the way that you like most.

I played in the LPO in 1938, when Szigeti premiered the new Bloch Concerto. It was lovely playing, and very exciting. I preferred this performance to his recording of the work. His vibrato varied from one day to the other, and sometimes became a bit lumpy. I once arrived half an hour early before a concert of his at the Queens Hall; he was playing a Mozart concerto and the Chausson **Poème**. I heard him practising a long run about forty times. The performance was most eloquent.

In the early 1950s I heard him give a magical recital in the newly built Royal Festival Hall. I remember particularly the Schubert **Rondo Brillante**. Sometimes he used quite personal bowings, which he called 'de luxe', because they created effects which added to the magic.

Before this concert, Max Rostal told all his pupils to hear this 'noble musician with an obsolete and faulty technique'. Rostal sat in the eighth row, looking through opera glasses. He was quite annoyed by the review of the concert in the Strad magazine which spoke of a wonderful recital. It said how gratifying it was to see Professor Rostal watching through opera glasses, so as to learn from him!

I remember reading an article which said that Szigeti was trying to ensure his own immortality and to make certain that none of his recordings would ever be deleted.

I didn't meet him until he was about seventy, when I visited him at his home in Vevey, near Geneva. He was very pleased that I knew all his recordings. While I was there, a parcel arrived for him, sent by a Dutch pupil. He opened it and found his 78 records of the **Baal Shem Suite** by Bloch. He said 'Do you mind if I put on a movement of this? It's been about twenty-five years since I made it, and I can't remember what it's like'. Then, as he listened, he exclaimed 'What eloquence—what young player of today would dare to play like that? Players are now so geared up to the microphone, that they're terrified to lift the bow off the string and come down with a wallop somewhere, for fear of making a scratch.'

BRONISLAW HUBERMAN 1882–1947

Huberman had the most extraordinary inner depths of perception. A most remarkable and wonderful artist—in some ways he had more charisma than anyone else. I remember, as a boy, going to concerts of his at the Queens Hall in which the audience stood up to applaud him. This didn't happen very often in England, although it was common in Germany.

Somehow, these qualities transcended the particular technique he had been taught—it was very much of the older school. He had enormous portamenti in his playing, which can be heard in his recordings of Lalo's **Symphonie Espagnole** and the Tchaikovsky Concerto. I

Bronislaw Huberman

remember hearing him play the Beethoven Concerto, and being a little mystified by how he played with virtually no vibrato in the slow movement. However, it was incredibly effective; there was fine bow control and sound production—just a great musician playing.

I once asked the distinguished teacher, Maxim Jacobsen, which was his favourite memory out of all the violinists he'd ever heard. He considered it to be Huberman as a boy. He said that Huberman had been an extraordinary prodigy in his early years, possessing certain magical qualities that later he didn't have; in particular, a wonderful sound. At the age of twelve he played the Brahms Concerto in Berlin, with Brahms in the audience. The story goes that afterwards Brahms came round to congratulate him. Huberman said 'I'm sorry that people clapped such a long time after the first movement.' Brahms replied 'You shouldn't have played the cadenza so well!'

How was it to work with him personally? I had a few lessons from him when I was fourteen and fifteen. I'd won a scholarship that was given in his name, at the Academy, so he was interested in how I was progressing. I played my odd bits and pieces to him and he just made a few remarks. I remember him saying 'Always try to make a sound of a high quality, whatever you're doing. Don't just play anything carelessly, but try to do everything well'. Also he said 'Challenge your fourth finger, to make it very strong'. He played me scales just on the third and fourth fingers, up and down a couple of octaves on the G string, as an exercise to encourage those fingers to work.

Huberman was the first major violinist to play on four metal strings. He wanted to play as strongly as possible. *Four metal strings can actually strangle the sound of a violin—adding tension can be counterproductive. You think you're getting more sound, but you're just choking it.* If you use four metal strings, the bridge should be about 1.5mm lower, so as to diminish the tension. Certainly, he made a magnificent sound on his Guarnerius. This violin was subsequently owned by Ruggiero Ricci.

The inventor of these strings, Dr. Thomastik, also invented, in 1930, a substitute for bow hair. Huberman used to play on twelve to fifteen flat strands of aluminium. He had the frogs of both his Tourtes modified to accommodate this. *It would have been preferable to have had alternative frogs made for the bows while he was using this system.* In those days one didn't think of that. A Tourte cost hundreds rather than thousands. An ordinary re-hair cost, in Hills, the equivalent of 12p. To have your bow fitted with the aluminium strips cost about £3. In the early 1930s you could buy a high grade Hill bow for £3.

ADOLF BUSCH 1891–1951

Adolf Busch was one of my great formative influences. *You didn't study with him at all?* No, but I heard him in concerts just after the war. Busch played in the older, more Germanic style. It was very forthright; you could say that it was quite like Huberman's playing, except that he played with a small, quite fast vibrato, sometimes with audible shifts.

No other quartet leader played the Beethoven quartets with such tremendous intensity. The way he played Beethoven and Schubert seemed to be telling me the truth about these great works.

There are many works where charm and seductive tonal beauty are imperative: this is not the case with late Beethoven. I always said

Adolph Busch
(Courtesy Tully Potter Collection)

that the Busch Quartet playing Beethoven was like a Chaplin film, grainy black and white. If you modified these films, by taking all the grain out, they wouldn't be so marvellous. Busch was a fantastic player; his bow control was utterly amazing, and he was a master of the retake. You could see him go along the bow and retake without any extraneous sound.

Through the years, I've always asked pupils of mine to listen to records of the Busch Quartet. I used to insist that they played some of these movements several times, until they appreciated the wonderful music making and got used to the slightly grainy playing by Busch. I remember being enchanted by the 1937 quartet recordings of Beethoven and Schubert. I found their Mozart and Haydn a little too heavy for my liking. I felt similarly about Klemperer's interpretations of these composers.

I was thrilled when they did a series of all the Beethoven string quartets, in five or six concerts, at the Chelsea Town Hall. The tickets were quite expensive. At the end of the first concert, the flautist

John Francis said 'Did you enjoy it?' I replied 'Yes, I thought it was quite wonderful music-making'. He said 'Well, I've bought tickets for the whole series and you can have them if you want.' *Was the playing too heavy for him?* I think he found it too old-fashioned.

Busch came here each year and used to do all the Brandenbergs and Bach suites with his chamber orchestra. It was the only time I've seen, in the Bach Flute Suite, the soloist sitting down and the leader standing. When I first played Brandenburg No.4 I used his very fast tempi, not having heard any other version.

Enescu and Menuhin

GEORGE ENESCU 1881–1955

Did you ever hear Enescu play? At one of the summer schools he played a little Bach. By then, in his seventies, he had a tremendously curved spine. *But did you hear enough to get a distinct impression?* Yes, I was amazed by the quality of his playing, although he looked to be in such an uncomfortable shape. When you're in your twenties you get general impressions of people—we thought he was a wonderful old man. We went to see him after the performance. I remember the way he held his beautiful Strad—he had his hand on the wood of the back and the belly. I noticed that the varnish was worn down in places.

His recordings of the Bach Sonatas and Partitas are exceptionally fine. In Bach he would always be saying 'Don't play the prestos too fast'. In the last movement of the Solo Sonata in G minor, his approach is the opposite to Milstein's more direct virtuoso approach. Enescu treats it melodically and there are many more colours and shades of expression. There are two ways of playing solo Bach fast movements: one is interestingly and musically inflected, the other fast and flawlessly.

His recording of the Chausson **Poème** is the most beautiful that I know; it has a luscious, sonorous tone.

I worked a lot with him just after the war with the Boyd Neel Orchestra, playing the Brandenburg Concertos, the Bartok **Divertimento** and his own **Octet**. *Was he conducting?* Yes—he was a wonderful musician.

I remember at one concert Walter Gieseking was playing the Mozart D Minor Piano Concerto. Enescu didn't like him, considering him to be a Nazi type. They had quite a fearful row over the last movement because Geiseking wanted to play it so fast. Enescu once said 'At my age I like to hear music both vertically and horizontally'—he didn't

George Enesco with Myron Grindea (l.) and Solomon (r.)

like breakneck speeds. Also, he wanted the difficult bassoon solo in the the Finale to be playable.

One thing I remember particularly about Enescu was his conducting of the Brandenburg Concertos. John Francis was playing the flute, the young Thurston Dart the harpsichord and the orchestra was led by Maurice Clare. John Francis was a good early music man: he didn't have a music stand, but had a big chair with the Bach Geselschaft open on it. At one point, Enescu said that there shouldn't be a slur. Francis said 'In the Geselschaft . . .' and Enescu interrupted 'What date is your Geselschaft?' It turned out to be the edition of thirty years earlier; Enescu said 'Wrong Geselschaft!'

YEHUDI MENUHIN 1916–1999

Menuhin studied with Enescu in his early years. *Did you hear him much in his younger days?* The first time I heard him he was eighteen and I was fifteen. My first impression was the sheer size of his tone. It was the biggest I have ever heard, with a wonderful quality, quite magical. He had a beautifully logical musical expression, coupled with an infallible technique.

His was really wonderful playing, the flexibility and rubato nearly always more poetic than anyone else. It pulled you straight away into the mood of whatever he played.

I heard him give two or three recitals with his sister, Hepzibah, in 1934. *How different was he in those days?* He said that by the time he was fifty he was remembering what it had been like, as a boy, to have had the sheer joy of the music, and the unquestioning knowledge that all his machinery was working perfectly. He told me how, at that time, he made some recordings with Hepzibah: the **Kreutzer** Sonata, one of the Schumann sonatas and the B minor Schubert **Rondo Brillante**. They went into the EMI studios, warmed up for five minutes and recorded immediately.

I made all my students listen to these records, to appreciate the imagination, musicianship and sensitivity Menuhin had when he was young. He was a fantastic violinist and a wonderfully instinctive musician.

I remember him coming to the Aldeburgh Festival in 1957. One of

Yehudi Menuhin with Benjamin Britten

the concerts he played included both the Debussy Sonata and the Schubert **Fantasy** with Benjamin Britten, which came out on CD only about a year ago. This is one of the greatest performances of the Schubert.

However, in his thirties and forties he was already having some problems. I still think that, on a good day, he was the greatest instinctive musician of them all. Then, when he started getting more problems, the playing got a little bit hysterical. The vibrato was never tight or ugly, but was very fast. He said of himself 'I'm a Russian Jewish violinist—I just play with instinct'.

I played the Mozart **Concertone**, for two solo violins, with Menuhin in the Aldeburgh Festival, at Blythbrough church. The concert was recorded for the BBC World Service, but couldn't be used because there was a thunderstorm during the performance.

Oistrakh, Stern and Kogan

There can be differences between players of the same school, as well as between different schools? I think the two greatest violinists of the Soviet Union, in the last fifty or sixty years, were David Oistrakh and Leonid Kogan; both had superlative techniques. Oistrakh always made a warm sound, while Kogan, to me, was a cool player—they were after different things.

DAVID OISTRAKH 1908–1974

I heard Oistrakh play the Tchaikovsky Concerto at the Albert Hall, when he first came to England in the late 1940s. This was great playing, but in a very different style to Heifetz. The fastest and most difficult passages were always full of tone and he used a much broader spiccato; there was immense solidity in the playing and a total mastery.

I remember that, on this visit, there was a reception given for him in the Guildhall. He was speaking through an interpreter. His violin was a famous Strad that had four black cracks on the front, two on each side—Russian repairs, but the fiddle sounded marvellous.

Eric Gruenberg asked him what bows he used. His answer was 'We are not incredibly rich people as musicians in the Soviet Union, but I've got four very serviceable bows'. He had two gold mounted Nürnbergers from around 1930, and two bows that came from a Russian shop called Kittel—nobody knows who made these bows. *Kittel was a shop?* Yes, there's so much controversy about him. *Did he make the bows or import them from France?* Well I've seen various ones: some are beautiful Tourty sort of bows while others look German. He must have made the frogs, because they are all rather alike, with big heavy silver rings.

The person who most influenced the young Oistrakh musically was Szigeti, whom he had heard play in Moscow. It was clear that

David Oistrakh
(*Courtesy Tully Potter Collection*)

Szigeti had certain technical problems, but what he did with the music was enchanting and magical. Oistrakh said that when he heard him he realised that his own aim shouldn't be just to play faster and more brilliantly.

There was a fine, unhurried sense of timing in Oistrakh's phrasing and remarkable beauty of sound. Any technical demand was met without losing breadth of tone; it was majestic in its total command. I always recommend students to watch videos of his playing to observe a perfect mechanism.

When did you first hear him? When I was still in the army in 1944, a four record set of the Khatchaturian Concerto came from Russia. It was made in 1937, after he'd won the big competition in Brussels. This was absolutely magnificent playing, although I thought the work merely a pleasant, rather protracted piece of light music. In 1946, while on tour in Europe, we went to East Berlin, which one could still visit. Records were very cheap and I remember buying one of him playing a concerto by Rakov, now a deservedly forgotten work. At the time it was proudly announced as having won a second Stalin prize.

There is a tape of Oistrakh playing the Mozart A major Concerto, on his first trip to the USA in the late 1940s. It is wonderful playing, but very much in the old Russian way. His style had changed by the early '50s; I heard him playing Mozart beautifully—but by then he'd been around in Europe for quite a while. I have a video of him rehearsing the tutti of the Mozart D major Concerto: he is telling the orchestra all the right things. The sheer perfection and transparency of Mozart makes his music difficult to play well. Schnabel said that teachers use Mozart for very young students, because there are not many notes: by contrast, virtuosi find that there aren't enough notes to keep them fully occupied. They have all this technique and want to be using it. However, speed and accuracy are just aspects of technique.

ISAAC STERN 1920–2001

Stern was born in Russia and went to the USA a year later. He was one of the greatest violinists. His magnificent playing in the Stern, Rose and Istomin Trio showed that he was a rarity—a genuine virtuoso talent with deep musicality and a special feeling for great music.

Stern was a man of wide influence, who was able to persuade a number of millionaires to save New York's Carnegie Hall—a treasured cultural institution.

When did you first hear him? The first time he came to England was in the late '50s. He played the Sibelius Concerto and the **Symphonie Espagnole** quite marvellously. I was then busy observing the bowing of great players, in particular how they changed at the heel. I was intrigued to find that I could see virtually no movement at all in Stern's fingers or wrist. I noticed that the point of the bow was going up and down in an arc (see page 144).

One of my favourite recordings is his 1953 Schubert Quintet, with Pablo Casals. This performance is marvellous—he was then about thirty. Recently I got a Bell Telephone Company Hour recording of 1959. The first item on that was Stern playing the Saint-Saëns **Rondo Capriccioso**. This is really like Heifetz. It's a super talent—playing of great ease, free of the need to care about exactness. His playing, as a young man, had more beauty of sound than it did later on—this is

Isaac Stern
(Courtesy Tully Potter Collection)

something I also felt about Mischa Elman. It may be to do with the fact that they both had similar hand shapes, with comparatively short fat fingers.

LEONID KOGAN 1924–1982

Kogan had such an amazing security of technique and sense of authority that he produced very fine performances, although he was not an interpreter of great subtlety. His tone quality was relentlessly beautiful, though sometimes a little hard. When on tour in the USA, I saw the newspaper headline of a review by Harold Schonberg, 'Kogan freezes Carnegie Hall'. He gave some masterclasses at the Julliard School and was similar to Heifetz, in that he was very demanding in his approach to scale practise, wanting scales in four octaves in every key.

The Flesch School

CARL FLESCH 1873–1944

I first heard Flesch perform as soloist when I was in the Scottish Orchestra with Szell. *How do you remember his playing?* I thought it was terrific. He played the **Fantasy** by Suk, a favourite piece of his which is not often performed. It is a romantic concerto in one movement lasting twenty minutes. It has an absolutely wonderful start, but then goes on a bit. His recording of this piece has been reissued on CD.

As an encore, he played Paganini's Caprice No. 20 really immaculately. It was really impressive fiddle playing.

I also heard him in 1938 in a charity concert with Schnabel. There were about forty people in a drawing room in St John's Wood and they raised several thousand pounds. As a student I got in for nothing. Flesch and Schnabel were long-term musical partners. Together they edited the Mozart sonatas. Flesch's son wrote a book that includes some of their correspondence about tempi and phrasing

Did you ever meet Flesch? No, but he was teaching in England and I knew many of his pupils. *You didn't attend one of his master classes?* No. I was studying at the Royal Academy and felt it would be wrong to go to another teacher. When I saw my friends again after the war, I found that several of them had gone to Flesch and had learnt a great deal from him.

What were the most obvious features of their progress? They all felt that they were able to practise in a much more productive way, because they knew what they were looking for. *He taught good organisation?* Oh, totally; it was all about technique.

How much did he teach music? It's an interesting question, because one of his great pupils was Ida Haendel, who'd been with him from the age of eleven or twelve. She wrote a book called **Woman with Violin**, in which she describes studying one summer with Enescu in Paris. Flesch found it rather hurtful that she'd felt she

Carl Flesch
(Courtesy Tully Potter Collection)

needed to study with someone else. She said that Enescu was only making musical demands, about phrasing, line and variations of tone quality and vibrato. He never once talked to her about technique—what part of the bow to use, ways of shifting or anything to do with posture. Yet at the end of those few weeks, somehow her technique was working even better!

This is very revealing, because technique is inseparable from music. There's a famous American team, working together for some years, a husband and wife. One of them talks about technique and the other about music. If you ask people to do certain things musically, you'll find that it is encouraging them to use their technique in a more subtle way. This subtlety is an important aspect of technique.

MAX ROSTAL 1905–1991

In 1948 I heard Rostal play the Dvorak Concerto at the Proms and thought it was very fine playing. Arnold Schoenberg probably would have thought that his sound was unchaste, as he did of the Budapest Quartet. It was very Viennese and rather schmaltzy. In 1970 I was leading the Philharmonia when Rostal broadcast the Benjamin Frankel Concerto and, two weeks later, that composer's Viola Concerto, played with the same effortless mastery on a large viola. I also heard him play an excellent Bartok Violin Concerto No. 2.

He was a great violinist, but his playing did not give me much pleasure. I sent several advanced pupils to him, although I knew that they would all be expected to use his bowings and fingerings—only a minority of his pupils continued to use his particular technical solutions after they left him.

In 1949 I had a few lessons from him. He wanted me to be more disciplined about hand shapes when shifting to high positions. He was the first person to persuade me about the beneficial effects of slow practise. I had a strange habit of practising at high speed, so as to discover technical limitations.

Rostal wanted me to use a pad of the right size, so as not to hunch my left shoulder. I spent months getting used to this larger pad, but it just made my playing worse. Then I went to a recital of Heifetz; I was sitting behind him and was able to observe that he drew up his left arm and shoulder much as I did. After seeing this, I reverted to my own way, to be comfortable. Rostal's approach was to be as labour-saving as possible but, for me, he was too relaxed in everything—almost floppy.

Max Rostal
(Courtesy Tully Potter Collection)

How much did his playing have a strong personality and musical impulse? I respected his playing tremendously but it didn't grab me in the way that say, Kreisler, Szigeti and Huberman did, in their different ways.

JOSEPH WOLFSTAHL 1899–1931

Wolfstahl, Flesch's foremost pupil in Berlin, came to London on holiday when I was eleven. I heard him practising in a friend's house and was really shattered by hearing this enormous violin sound at close quarters. It was the first time I had heard a fine Stradivari in a room—quite a wonderful sound.

HENRI TEMIANKA 1906–1992

Temianka was a Polish Jew who, by chance, was born in Glasgow when his parents were attending a rabbinical conference. When I

Henri Temianka
(*Courtesy Tully Potter Collection*)

was playing in the Scottish Orchestra in 1938 I heard him play a marvellous Mendelssohn Concerto. His tone production had a beauty akin to that of Kreisler. In the same year he made a recording of the Schubert **Adagio and Rondo**, which I have always loved.

He was on tour in the USA in the spring of 1939. In the summer, while still there on holiday, he decided to stay. A wealthy American lady offered the use of her quartet of Strads for him to start a string quartet. The group was named the Paganini Quartet. To me, his playing in the quartet was innocently soloistic—rather lightweight but full of charm. Later on, he had a distinguished teaching career on the West Coast and was conductor of his own very successful chamber orchestra.

SZYMON GOLDBERG 1909–1993

I had a great regard for Szymon Goldberg, whom I considered an important musician. I enjoyed his playing more when he was a young man, feeling that he had become too pedantic in his old age.

Szymon Goldberg
(Courtesy Tully Potter Collection)

I respected him very much as a teacher—he was one of the few people in America who talked to students intelligently about bow distribution. If, in a chamber music competition, I heard a particularly fine American quartet leader, I'd usually find that this was a Goldberg pupil.

He was an excellent performer of the Mozart sonatas, which he recorded both with Lili Kraus in 1938 and with Radu Lupu in 1968.

He once visited me to ask my opinion of a Kittel bow he was thinking of buying. I remember that the dealer who was selling it wanted his Dominique Peccatte plus quite a lot of money for it. I advised him to keep his excellent Peccatte.

HENRYK SZERYNG 1918–1988

When I first heard Szeryng, I considered him to be a violinist of the first rank, with great technical accomplishment and a beautiful tone.

He was always delighted to impress. I remember a social gathering one evening, after he had played a concerto in London. It was a relaxed occasion with an excellent buffet, after which he needed little persuasion to bring out his fiddle. After some excellent solo Bach and a couple of Paganini caprices, he played the cadenza of the **Labyrinth Caprice** of Locatelli, which was quite new to me.

He gave a very fine recital with Norma Fisher in 1973; it was a fund-raising concert for Israel at the time of the war. He sailed up the G string quite effortlessly in the Brahms D minor Sonata.

I have always thought of Szeryng as a classical type of violinist. His performance of a recently discovered Paganini concerto was totally honourable rather than truly virtuoso. There is a recent video of two early performances. The Beethoven Concerto is distinguished; the Tchaikovsky Concerto has mechanical exactitude, but somehow lacks the tonal excitement I associate with this work.

He was always delighted to give master classes, in which he would demonstrate the points he was making. He was not tall, but well built for the violin, with no need of a shoulder rest.

He enjoyed a drink, but it didn't affect his playing. However, at a party when he consumed more than usual he would say 'Call me Henryk', and then ten minutes later 'Call me Mr. Szeryng'. He was friendly, but rather conscious of his status.

I was leading the Philharmonia when he recorded the Beethoven Triple with cellist Janos Starker and pianist Claudio Arrau. At one point during the session, after a discussion, they decided to repair to the listening room. Starker turned to the orchestra and said that a feature of this recording was the total lack of agreement between the soloists. Entering the control room, Szerying said 'Janos, you shouldn't have said that—think of the morale of the orchestra'. Starker replied 'Henryk, you were the only one who didn't laugh!'

JOSEPH HASSID 1923–1950

I heard Josef Hassid, another Flesch pupil, in rather unusual circumstances. I had gone to a house in St. Johns Wood to play to the **Jewish Educational Aid Society**. On arriving, I heard the Wieniawski Polonaise in D being played quite fantastically—pyrotechnics produced with effortless precision. This was a white-hot talent that could only be compared to Heifetz. As I came into the room, I was surprised to see a twelve-year-old boy playing. He had a Vuillaume violin, lent to him by Kreisler.

When he was eighteen, he made a few records. On hearing himself, he said he didn't realise that his vibrato sounded so fast—nobody had told him. He wanted to cool it a bit, so as to sound more relaxed.

IDA HAENDEL b.1928

I first heard Ida Haendel when she was officially fourteen, although she said she was really twelve at the time. I was playing in the LPO when she performed the Mozart G major Concerto. I thought it was stunning violin playing—a wonderful natural talent.

The next time I worked with her was in 1969. I was leading the Philharmonia when she played the Brahms Concerto. It was both majestic and poetic. She asked us just to give the impression of accompanying strongly when it is marked *f*, because she didn't want to have to force her sound.

Only a couple of years ago I heard her play a concerto, and she was still playing immaculately.

French and Belgian Violinists

JACQUES THIBAUD 1880–1953

I heard Thibaud play just one recital. The first half was quite terrible. Norbert Brainin was there and we were discussing in the interval whether or not to stay; many people were leaving. Then, in the second half, he really played marvellously. I didn't realise that he liked to have a good dinner with wine, and then play himself in during the first part of the concert, just as Kreisler did.

When I asked my father which was the most memorable musical performance that he had heard, he said it was Thibaud, accompanied by Harold Craxton, playing the **Havanaise** *at the Royal Academy of Music Club.* He could play wonderfully, rather like Kreisler, although without quite as much technique—he never played Paganini.

A recently released CD includes a characteristic performance of the Saint-Saëns **Rondo Capriccioso.**

GINETTE NEVEU 1919–1949

Just after the war, I was playing in the New London Orchestra. Ginette Neveu, less expensive before becoming a star, played the concertos of Beethoven and Brahms several times with us. *How was her sound and projection in public?* She made a very big, intense sound on her wonderful Strad, playing well into the string. Her Brahms was warm and full blooded. It was a smouldering sound.

I remember that at one rehearsal she broke her E string and the leader, Max Salpeter, offered her his fiddle, a very good Panormo. Immediately her tone shrank to about a quarter of its size. Percival Hodgson said that, if you play too intensely all the time, there may be little contrast in a really fiery passage. *Did you feel this about her?* I think so. On her recordings, her Brahms is wonderfully intense and so is her Sibelius. Perhaps her Debussy is too much so, as are her Kreisler solos. *Humour plays quite a part in Kreisler pieces.* Also in Schubert, Haydn, Mozart, and even in some Beethoven. The Scherzo of Beethoven's Quartet Op. 131 has got a wonderfully whistleable tune. When we played the work for BBC Television, the lighting engineers were whistling it afterwards.

ARTHUR GRUMIAUX 1921–1986

The first time I worked with Grumiaux was in 1947 in Bristol with the New London Orchestra, when he played the Brahms Concerto. The new concert manager of the orchestra was slightly self-important. He didn't yet know everybody and, when he saw Grumiaux strolling around the back, he insisted on him sitting down, pushing him into a seat in the second violins.

In the few times that I've heard him in concert, I've found that he didn't do anything in particular with the music; he just stood there and played. However, on his records he sounds really wonderful. He recorded a lot of chamber music: Mozart string quintets and the string trio and also Schubert's **Trout Quintet**, which came out at the same time as my recording of it with the Melos. Their version was compared with ours on the Saturday morning record review. The critic put on part of the Scherzo, making out that Grumiaux was technically uncomfortable in a certain passage, which was total rubbish.

He recorded Mozart concertos with the ECO, in the days before composite strings were widely used. He used to change his bottom strings in the evening, after the rehearsals, because he wanted a real sizzle in his sound. The next morning, the recording takes therefore had to be rather short, because his strings needed frequent tuning.

CHRISTIAN FERRAS 1933–1982

The first time I heard Ferras, he was playing the Bach Double with Menuhin. He was very short and sturdy, only about 5 ft 4 in. They gave him a two inch platform to stand on beside Yehudi. I thought Ferras was quite a wonderful player; I remember his big, generous sound. An exceptionally musical and gifted violinist—it was tragic that he was such a nervous person. He died of cirrhosis of the liver.

I heard him once, playing the Beethoven Concerto in Barcelona. It was very beautiful playing. There was a simplicity and directness in his musical line that went straight to the heart of the matter.

When I was in the Philharmonia in 1970, he came to play the Berg Concerto. He arrived at the rehearsal in the morning slightly under the influence of strong drink. He could still play wonderfully, even in that state. I've been listening recently to a wonderful CD of him playing lots of small tunes, and a fine performance of the **Symphonie Espagnole**. It is marvellous playing, but a little too 'correct' when compared to the 1934 record of Huberman, who really sounds like a bullfighter in the last movement.

There is a DVD now available of fine performances of the Sibelius and Stravinsky concertos.

Other Violinists

ALBERT SAMMONS 1886–1957

I heard fine performances by Sammons in the 1930s, but only got to know him somewhat later. He was a violinist who really served the music. There was a beautiful honesty of interpretation, with no extreme rubatos. His recordings of the Elgar and Delius concertos are of great stature. He told me that the Elgar was recorded in the winter and there was no heating in the studio.

I knew him towards the end of his life and helped him sell his violin when he retired. I also bought a Lamy bow from him.

TOSSI SPIVAKOVSKY 1907–1998

Spivakovsky was a fiery virtuoso of the highest class. I have his record of the Tchaikovsky Concerto, and an old 78 of him playing one of the Sarasate virtuoso pieces. When watching him play, it was hard to believe how he managed to do it. Everything was contrary to most people's idea of technique. The chin rest was on the side of the violin, and he used a high finger action, banging them down for greater articulation. He describes in his tutor how, over the years, violinists have gradually held the bow higher and higher on the first finger. His finger position is the highest of all, higher than Heifetz. He had an extraordinary claw-like bow hold, but he sounded quite wonderful.

MICHAEL RABIN 1936–1972

Rabin auditioned for Galamian at the Juilliard School when he was thirteen, playing five Paganini caprices. Galamian then asked Francescatti to hear him play. Francescatti used to think that there was no point in performing Paganini caprices unless one had grown up with them. After hearing Rabin he advised Galamian to get him to record them before he realised how difficult they were. One can hear the incredible quality of his technique in his complete recording of the Caprices. His playing has a certain innocence and freshness. This set is as fine as any I know. I heard him play the Tchaikovsky Concerto at the Maida Vale Studios. It was superlative violin playing but, ultimately, not as individual musically as Huberman or Elman.

I was very pleased when Rabin came to hear me play the Schubert **Adagio and Rondo** in Zurich. He was most complimentary, saying that I had made it sound very interesting. He said that he had not previously discovered this when examining the score.

Violinists I only Heard on Recordings

ALBERT SPALDING 1888–1953

Spalding's playing was very beautiful, but it didn't have quite the intensity of the Russian school.

EFREM ZIMBALIST 1889–1985

A violinist of the highest class, worthy to rank with the greatest. One of the most distinguished members of Auer's St. Petersburg class, he played with great technical assurance and noble musical instincts, without the eccentricity of Elman or the unbridled virtuosity of Heifetz. Sometimes I noticed a carefree approach to certain rhythmic figures that came from an age when players were less used to hearing their recorded performances. A splendid recent reissue of his Brahms Concerto, from a live performance in 1946, is coupled with the Brahms D minor Sonata of 1930.

VÁŠA PŘÍHODA 1900–1960

Příhoda had an extraordinary virtuoso flair and was very musical. It was not the icy perfection of Kogan, but slightly old fashioned playing with portamenti.

ZINO FRANCESCATTI 1902–1991

Francescatti was a violinist with an incomparable left hand. However, I found that his performances of some of the great concertos were not totally effective. He used his bow as something comfortable—it was travelling all the time. It just took away from the last bit of sheer musicality possible. His editions always have too many bow changes.

Just after he died, I saw a programme about his life on French television. When asked, in an interview, 'What are the most difficult works, or the ones that you have found to be a challenge?' he answered 'I can't think of anything in particular'.

He made a wonderful record of the Walton Concerto. People say that nobody plays this work like Heifetz, but I think that Francescatti's record is comparable.

The Past, Present and Future

It is natural for people to play in a manner that relates to the time they live in. In 2006 life is different from 1950, even more from 1900. A few years ago, the Royal Shakespeare Company gave a class for young actors. They showed an excerpt from Laurence Olivier's **Henry V**, which is wonderful acting of its time, but they said that no young actor would want to do it the same way today.

In the last fifty years, standards of technical tuition and the sheer amount of practice done by students has tended to iron out individuality. The unique qualities of some wonderful players of the past relate, to some extent, to their individual approach to solving certain technical problems; thus I have felt it more relevant to concentrate here on the great violinists of my earlier years.

Today, teaching in various countries is becoming more uniform; the different schools concentrate on similar basic approaches to technique. There has been an increasing number of first-class violinists over the last forty years, partly because more students are being well taught.

An analogy exists in that today there are many successful violin makers. They are not so much divided into distinct schools as they were in the past. Instruments in the Italian or French style are made in many parts of the world.

Great players of the past were always eager to play chamber music whenever possible. Many young players of today are almost totally innocent of this repertoire. Music colleges generally don't give enough time to chamber music.

The first benefit from playing chamber music is an introduction to a great and profound repertoire. There is only one concerto by Beethoven, but seventeen string quartets. Mozart's concertos were written when he was still in his teens, but his great quartets and quintets date from his mature years. At least thirty of the Haydn quartets are far greater music than the two violin concertos. Apart from a couple of solos, Schubert's contribution to the repertoire is in his chamber music; Brahms also wrote a wonderful variety of chamber music.

Then there is the discipline that chamber music brings, of having to play in a more controlled and rhythmic manner. If a soloist hurries a passage, a conductor will move forward accordingly. In a quartet, the others will expect it to be in time and, if it is not, will complain vigorously.

Physically and technically, each member of a quartet, but mainly the first violinist, must learn how to give leads. This is something that is harder when a shoulder rest is used. I feel that if I am leading a Haydn quartet which my colleagues don't know, I should be able to play and lead well enough for them to grasp the phrasing and direction of the music.

In chamber music there is the need for many different tone colours, types of vibrato, finger shapes, lengths of spiccato and bowing styles. By contrast, over the last forty years, there has been a tendency to use vibrato rather thoughtlessly and indiscriminately. This takes away the possibility of varying the musical stress when shaping a phrase. To phrase with distinction, it is essential to be able to control and vary the amount and type of vibrato on different notes.

The benefits from chamber music are incalculable. Most significantly, it contributes towards the development of true musicality. A soloist who is also a fine chamber music player will play concertos with a greater musical depth.

Composers

Benjamin Britten
(Courtesy Tully Potter Collection)

ZOLTÁN KODÁLY 1882–1967

Zoltán Kodály was very friendly when working with us. He was a quiet and gentle person. I was playing at Aldeburgh his Duo for Violin and Cello with Keith Harvey, and also his String Trio for two violins and viola with Ivor McMahon and Cecil Aronowitz. We had breakfast with him on the morning of the concert and then played him these works. He suggested one tempo modification, but otherwise seemed pleased. His choir sang a number of his folk songs in the concert. Afterwards, Britten said to him 'That last song was absolutely heart rending; what are the words?' Kodály replied 'The peasant eats his cheese'.

ARTHUR BLISS 1891–1975

The music of Arthur Bliss is rather neglected nowadays. He wrote a very fine ballet, **Checkmate**, a film score for H.G.Wells' **Things To Come** and a very good string quartet. I used to play both his Clarinet Quintet and his Oboe Quintet with the Melos, and we recorded these works. I'm sorry that these recordings are no longer available, because they were good performances.

The Strad magazine recently was talking about the string orchestra repertoire. The article mentioned a number of pieces that most orchestras know nothing about. I was quite amazed to see that it left out a piece by Bliss called **Music for Strings**, which lasts about twenty minutes. It is an absolutely top-class string orchestra work, comparable to the **Introduction and Allegro** of Elgar. If I hadn't been so lazy, I'd have written and complained to the magazine about this omission.

PAUL HINDEMITH 1895–1963

I accompanied Paul Hindemith when playing in the Scottish Orchestra under Georg Szell in 1937. Hindemith played his own Viola Concerto called **Schwanendrehrer** in the first half, and the solo part of **Harold in Italy** after the interval. We were rather intrigued that he performed this work using two music stands. He considered that he wasn't busy enough just playing the solo part: so he had the first violin tutti part beside him to play on his viola, along with the first violin section.

In the 1950s, with the Goldsborough Orchestra, we broadcast with him his own sad, short requiem piece, **Trauermusik**, that he had written in a morning for King George the Fifth's funeral. We also played his third and fifth quartets, which I found very brilliant pieces. A movement of the third quartet is short and virtuosic, scored just for viola and cello, so the two violins enjoy three minutes of not doing anything. *He also wrote a duo for this combination. Has this quartet movement ever been used by viola and cello players as a piece in its own right?* I don't think I've ever been to a viola and cello recital. *We used to search for such pieces, to give variety to baryton trio programmes.*

How subtle was Hindemith as a player? When he played the viola in the post-war years, he was not all that well in practice. I think that he saw these performances just as part of his income.

When Norbert Brainin played to him, he had just wanted his music very bright, fast and breezy: he wasn't really interested in Norbert's inner thoughts about the music.

There are recordings of his two string trios, which he played with Szymon Goldberg and Emanuel Feuermann. His playing definitely sounds of the older school; it's not particularly ingratiating. I've got a record of him playing one of his solo pieces, which is not very beautiful sounding music. My greatest memory of him was the concert of 1937.

ALAN BUSH 1900–1995

The music of Alan Bush is nowadays undeservedly neglected, although there is an Alan Bush Society, which is recording a number of his works. He taught me keyboard harmony at the RAM. Later, in the army in 1942, I was surprised to find him working in the RAMC. I played some concerts with a string orchestra, which included a version of his one movement string quartet called **Dialectic**. I was very pleased to hear the Medici Quartet's recording of this piece. For me, this is an important contribution to the string quartet literature.

AARON COPLAND 1900–1990

Did you ever meet Aaron Copland? Yes, every year Britten invited a different composer to take part in his festival. I've got a photograph of myself, at an Aldeburgh Festival, holding the score of Copland's Piano Quartet which we played with the Melos. Another piece that we played was his own reduction of his Clarinet Concerto, for a chamber group. I found his music really wonderful—in a way like Stravinsky, but more difficult. *What were your personal memories of him?* He came to listen to us and said we played well. He made one or two suggestions about tempi and things, but he wasn't particularly warm to work with. *Have you ever played his Violin Sonata?* No, but I think it is a good piece. *He speaks of it as virtually his simplest work.*

WILLIAM WALTON 1902–1983

Around 1960, while playing in the London Piano Quartet, our viola player, Watson Forbes, discovered a copy of an early piano quartet by William Walton. This was his first published composition, written in 1918–19. We liked the work and contacted the composer who came to hear us rehearse it. He said that he found the work less embarrassing than he had expected, but wanted to make a few changes. I remember how he completely transformed the fugue subject of the last movement just by taking out one note. Later on, with the Aeolian Quartet, we played for him his String Quartet, at a dinner at the Garrick Club in honour of his seventieth birthday.

LENNOX BERKELEY 1903–1989

I enjoyed playing with Lennox Berkeley. I used to like playing his String Trio, also a piece for string orchestra. When we played it at a concert in Scotland, I heard a voice in the audience saying, 'As I thought, it's more of this modern music again.' His son, Michael Berkeley, is now a well-known composer.

BERTHOLD GOLDSCHMIDT 1903–1996

Goldschmidt moved to London in 1935 after his music was banned in Germany, but he ceased composing in 1958, following neglect by the establishment. I first knew him as an excellent conductor who did some work with the ECO. In the 1980s he reappeared dramatically as a successful and fashionable composer. I heard his Violin Concerto, which was written in a post-Reger style. It is very proficient; still tonal, but rather congested.

MICHAEL TIPPETT 1905–1998

I found it interesting working with Michael Tippett; I think some of his works are very great. However, he had so many ideas going on at once that a lot of his music is, I think, too prolix. It's like having three or four Max Reger fugues going at the same time. He was a rather dangerously risky conductor. If something fell apart when he was rehearsing, he would just be very amused. His **Fantasia on a Theme of Corelli** for strings has two very prominent solo violin parts; it is very complicated, but a wonderful piece. I have never yet heard his last string quartet. The two that I've played, the first and second, are in their way perhaps more difficult than the Bartok Quartets—they are so complex. I very much admire the way the Lindsay Quartet play them. They worked at length with Tippett, really assimilating these very difficult pieces and they presented them marvellously.

I consider his Triple Concerto to be a major addition to the repertoire and wish it were performed more often.

ALAN RAWSTHORNE 1905–1971 & BERNARD STEVENS 1916–1983

Alan Rawsthorne and Bernard Stevens were both tonal composers, which was rather unfashionable. Rawsthorne had some success after the war with his **Symphonic Studies**, and I always enjoyed his Violin Sonata and his fine string quartets. Bernard Stevens wrote an excellent Violin Concerto, and two string quartets.

BENJAMIN BRITTEN 1913–1976

I worked regularly with Benjamin Britten from 1946, up to the time that I left the English Chamber Orchestra. I also played with him in the Aldeburgh Festival until 1968, so it was a long association. He was a really wonderful musician to play for, yet an ultrasensitive man who could be easily hurt. At a rehearsal, just after hearing him conduct the London Symphony Orchestra, I told him how enjoyable his performance had been. He said 'Yes, but it's really nerve-wracking working with one of those orchestras—I much prefer working with my own friends'.

As a conductor, he was not overly histrionic. His rehearsals were totally concerned with phrasing and balance. He would ask for a particular tone colour—something quite rare for a conductor. We all recognised him as an important musician. Somehow, every performance was an event—none was routine.

Did his sensitivity make him a bit difficult about certain things? He was mainly oversensitive about everyone knowing that he had a homosexual relationship, which in those days was less acceptable. Recently there was the centenary of William Walton. I remember Walton coming to Aldeburgh to conduct his opera, **The Bear**. Walton was a good old-fashioned heterosexual, and he used to call the place Aldebugger, although he was ostensibly very friendly. *I suppose Britten was very sensitive to such things?* Tremendously sensitive. I know that there was one very famous conductor who complained irritably about there being too many bloody boys around. He wasn't asked back the following year.

Was there a fairly high turnover of personnel at Aldeburgh? There were quite a number of famous people who were never asked back. I was one of the few people who actually resigned, instead of getting the sack. *But you'd had a long innings there?* Oh, very much so. When I resigned, I had the pleasure of going to Britten's home, the **Red House**. He wanted me to continue and couldn't quite understand why I was leaving.

BRUNO MADERNA 1920–1973

I knew Bruno Maderna in the 1960s. He was a composer who sometimes mixed live music and tapes. I first met him in 1961 at Dartington, when he was conducting the Melos Ensemble in a

Kay Hurwitz

Bruno Maderna

Mozart divertimento. He was the only avante garde composer who ever helped me with Mozart phrasing. We recorded with him, for Decca, two works of Schoenberg: the **Septet** and the **Serenade**.

LUIGI NONO 1924–1990

I played a work by Luigi Nono for the BBC which had several sopranos carefully dotted around the platform. There were two or three percussion players with small cymbals tied to their left arms. Nono was a wealthy left-winger. I heard his opera **Intoleranza** in the Fenice Theatre in Venice. It was a 1960s mixture of explosive percussion sounds with a back projection of riots. It was given a second night—the first had been barracked by a right wing protest in the gallery.

LUCIANO BERIO 1925–2003

I worked with Berio on a flute work written for Severino Gazzaloni. I remember him as lively and very amiable.

HANS WERNER HENZE b.1926

Hans Werner Henze wrote a song cycle for Peter Pears, which was accompanied by Julian Bream and the nine players of the Melos Ensemble—quite a substantial piece. I heard several of his works and felt that his music was always graceful and lyrical, if not particularly memorable.

KRZYSZTOF PENDERECKI b.1933, WITOLD LUTOSLAWSKI 1913–1994 & ALEXANDER GOEHR b.1932

In the early 1960s, association with the Italian School took the Melos to a lot of contemporary music festivals. In Warsaw we performed the Schonberg Septet. Penderecki and Lutowslawski conducted their own new works. I also remember Alexander Goehr conducting his music there. We also went twice to the Zagreb Festival, playing contemporary works. At one concert, as we started, there was a flash from a photographer and we all got lost. Fortunately, it was just before a General Pause bar and the ensemble righted itself.

Bach and Authenticity

Declan J. Ryan

Discussion with the author

Can we talk today about Bach's music for violin and the general subject of authenticity? Let's start by considering the variety of approaches used in Bach editions. In the time of the composer, violinists used mainly the lower positions, which involved a lot of string crossing techniques. I remember recently comparing three editions of the Sonatas and Partitas, just to see how different violinists solved the problems. *What are your views about the bowings in the manuscript, from the viewpoint of a performing edition?* There has been a lot of development of violin technique since the eighteenth century. It would be a pity not to make use of some of these changes, so long as the phrase is not distorted. It's very fashionable these days to use a lot of separate bows in Bach slow movements, because there are not very many slurs in the manuscript. The older editions put in some extra slurs, which can often be helpful. If we think of the slow movements of the A minor and C major Solo Sonatas, I think that there are various groups of two notes where a slur can be inferred from a parallel passage.

What effect do you think that extra slurs have on the enunciation of a melody? The slurs make the tune more legato; of course it's a moot point how Bach would have played it. Bach often said that his music should be as legato as possible—this was difficult, because in those days keyboard fingering was much more primitive. Gunther Kehr's preface to Szeryng's edition of the solo works of Bach considers some of the technical, musical and stylistic problems. There are very few clues as to how Bach played. There are many more about Mozart—we know that he was always stressing the need for legato when rehearsing, saying that his music must flow like oil. He didn't like the chopped up playing of the older musicians around him. Mozart was asking for, and playing, legato according to his own standards. The young Beethoven, who heard him play, said that it was phenomenal, but a bit too cut up.

It can be difficult to know where Bach wanted slurs in his violin lines. I have often played Bach cantatas from original editions. There are instances when the chorus has a melody with slurs over three syllables—three notes. When the wind has the same line, Bach sometimes puts the same slurs in their parts, but puts nothing in the string parts. It is very likely that he left certain things to copyists and didn't put the articulation in every part. Sometimes Bach only had a rather weak string section available for the Sunday service. On these occasions he would lead the orchestra himself on the violin, instead of playing the harpsichord or the organ, thus keeping better order by playing firmly. *Styles were changing during the lifetimes of these composers?* Very much. Towards the end of Bach's life, the fortepiano was invented. It is said that Bach was tremendously impressed by this new instrument, and considered it a very important development. Within a short time the piano became more popular than the harpsichord. People found it had so many more possibilities. More recently there was a parallel to this, when a well-known specialist in the early piano decided he would henceforth play Bach on a modern piano, thus contradicting the whole of his earlier career by doing so.

* * * * *

One can see today three different approaches to Bach. We have people using so-called baroque instruments and others playing in a totally modern way. In between there are those using modern instruments but influenced, to a greater or lesser extent, by recent trends in baroque playing. *There is often the danger in this third approach of not using the full resonance of the instrument. Do you have views on the partial baroque approach?* I know that, for example, a dotted quaver plus semiquaver passage, in the baroque days, was automatically played: ⊓ V⊓ V⊓ Apparently they used to play it in the lower part of the bow—nowadays specialists would consider it the greatest heresy to play this rhythm using both ends of the bow: ⊓ ⊓V V⊓

These specialists have become so influential that you can hear this approach being used even in Brahms or Tchaikovsky symphonies, although that music was written over a hundred years later. So in dotted passages, where wind and strings are in unison, the wind players will be giving fuller value to the longer notes than the strings.

When the modern bow was developed, around 1760, it became possible to play strongly at either end. The good players were very enthusiastic about this. Players today should be able to use both ends of the bow, making them sound virtually the same. This is very important, because to play V⊓ at the the heel or ⊓V at the point, are two very different activities. It is vital to be able to make both work well. Perhaps one of these old composers, if around nowadays, would be horrified that we are still hamstrung by limitations of the old bows of his day. The opposite view is also possible—that we are distorting the music through the use of different, i.e. modern, bowing technique.

One of Milstein's favourite encores was the last movement of Bach's C major Sonata. He sometimes used extra slurs, to facilitate string crossings and the brilliance of the writing—this was done by many great players of his time. I used to tell pupils, who used urtext phrasing as bowings, that they would never be able to play it as wonderfully as Milstein. *You are speaking about a need to supplement the slurs in the copy, particularly when crossing strings, so as to get the bow working better on the instrument?* Yes.

How would this work in the Preludio of the E major Partita? It's very fashionable now to play that just as it's written, which means you're often doing ⊓V, instead of V⊓. You have either the short or the long string crossing. It's very important to be aware of the techniques you need on those—I don't think it sounds as brilliant when played with the original bowing. *So you discreetly add a slur before a string crossing passage, in order to bring in the right up and down bow feeling?* I don't think one should even be discreet about it—it's a very brilliant prelude. *We are talking about the addition of a slur, so as to use the bow more naturally and effectively?* I think that making the technique as natural as possible helps to serve the musical values. The music is more important than theoretical ideas regarding authenticity, some of which change every few years anyway.

There are obviously different approaches to the planning of Bach articulation. One is to go via the manuscript, putting in any extra slurs as needed; the other is to explore the various editions for solutions that great players have discovered. Would you recommend a combination of both routes? It all depends on how long you have to explore these pieces. As regards articulation, quite often in Bach works you get the same passage coming back after seven or eight lines with different slurs on it—which thickens the plot. Also it's uncertain whether the slurs are bowings or phrasings.

The only Bach manuscript of the Cello Suites is by Anna Magdalena Bach and it is occasionally inaccurate. Other contemporary copies offer certain interesting points of comparison, but cellists often don't realise that they can find a mine of information in Bach's splendid manuscript of the solo violin works. It can help in keeping any necessary revisions of the original bowings in the Cello Suites within stylistic limits. How much credence do you give to the idea that the detaché stroke was the basic bowing style, slurs being used to pick out groups of notes? I think that most slurs are written to link notes which belong together harmonically. In a group of four notes, where three are part of the same chord, those three will have a slur. If the phrase is extended over all four notes, we may be smoothing out something which should have been phrased more distinctly. *What happens when the number of slurs is expanded?* Perhaps if we heard a good violinist of Bach's time playing one of his adagios, we wouldn't like it very much, finding it far removed from today's style of playing. I don't think one should play Bach melodies like Tchaikovsky, but there are other ways to be expressive. Regarding articulation notated by Bach in a movement, I'm assured that some of the clipping of second notes in a slur may be associated with the very primitive fingering techniques of keyboard players of the time. If they were very good artists, they might have been copied by string players as well.

But separate bows and slurred bows, on a violin or cello, are very different. To me this is a very important consideration for a string player. A first-class keyboard player might not play sixteen semiquavers in a bar the same as each other—some notes may be a little longer than others. If a baroque specialist said that this type of passage should be played only with separate bows, how would you answer that? Slurring is not the only way of creating variety. When in a chamber music class a piano trio is playing a work by Haydn, Mozart or Beethoven, I'll pick out a section of fast semiquavers and ask the pianist to play them and then another different passage. Then I will say to the class, 'You've heard two lots of semiquavers. Which passage has a slur written over them, and which one has no markings?' The point is that on the piano there's not so much difference, but if you hear a violinist playing sixteen notes in one bow, or sixteen notes with separate bows, the difference is very significant.

I've heard conscientious violinists, in Mozart sonatas, playing accompanying passages much less expressively than the pianist. In the big A major Sonata of Mozart K526, the last movement is very fast and brilliant. It's written in quavers, and there are several pages where the pianist plays this tune, with the violinist accompanying in crotchets. Then, eventually, the violin gets the tune, and it has a number of bowings: two slurred and two separates, and three slurred and one separate. These markings were added by Mozart, but they are not marked in the piano part. Why did he feel impelled to write these in the violin part? *Could it be that, for a particular performance, he knew what he wanted in his own part and just put markings in the violin part?* Well I'm not sure whether this piece was written for him or someone else—a lot of these works are written for other people as well. I remember hearing two very distinguished young artists playing one of my favourite Mozart sonatas. I was disturbed, right at the beginning, to find that the violinist sounded very unphrased. By the recapitulation I realised that an urtext edition was being used, with separate bows in what we'd always known as rather gracious passages.

So there's the concept of being overrespectful of the text, in the sense that it becomes an inhibition? One modern edition has published all the chamber music of Brahms. Brahms was happy with Simrock's editing, but a few late amendments by the composer were omitted. The urtext editions however usually go with Brahms' final thoughts.

Shortly before my first performance of the Bach G minor Solo Sonata, I came across the urtext. I found that it showed differences from the way it was played on the great recordings I had listened to. Certain bowings I had always heard and had played in the last movement were incorrect, and it was hard to learn different patterns. Nowadays I always show the urtext to my students.

* * * * *

Some years ago, a distinguished ex-Galamian American violinist was staying in my house while in London. He had recently become a baroque fanatic and was preparing Bach's D Minor Partita for a recording. I was listening in some anguish to his rather fast and, for me, too light approach. When I said to him 'Isn't this a little fast and small?' he replied, 'Yeah, you godda minify(!)' He believed that you should never use the top half of the bow. *Why?* Because, in all the old writings on the subject, they stress the use of the lower half. *How would you describe what he was doing and why it was small?* He was playing on a very fine Amati, which he'd had baroqued. He was using gut strings, an out-curved bow, and he was playing with a very low right elbow—*not his usual way of playing?* No. I'd heard him playing Paganini caprices, very comfortably, in the modern style. *Why was the sound much smaller in his Bach?* If you're playing a baroque violin with a flatter bridge, there is the danger of the bow touching the other strings. You can't play in a really big style, yet it is astonishing how strong a baroque violin can sound.

Would you say that those who play Bach on a modern violin, using a baroque style, tend to have a reduced volume level? At the Wigmore Hall recently I heard an international virtuoso start a recital with solo Bach. He was playing in a fairly informed early music style, which is somewhat smaller and lighter than a modern player. To me, it didn't sound as impressive as it could have sounded. When I was growing up, the idea, in playing the Bach Chaconne, was to make the violin sound like an organ. *A full vibration of the instrument?* Yes, of using the violin to its biggest capacity. *If one doesn't do that there's a danger of appearing emotionally cut off, of not using oneself as well as the instrument to the full.* These days it's considered correct for music colleges to have a specialist teaching the baroque violin. When visiting as an outside examiner, I often hear fourth-year and postgraduate students play a rather puny Bach Adagio, followed by a strong Tchaikovsky Concerto first movement. This shows the influence of the baroque specialist, but I don't think the students are learning a sufficiently holistic approach to Bach.

I think a lot of young people today are rather confused about how to play these works. The views are shifting all the time and each decade brings changes in opinion from the baroque camp. Certainly there's been a change in attitude towards sound since the beginning of the baroque revival. The sheer quality of sound is less considered, particularly when using a baroque violin. I have friends and colleagues who are distinguished baroque violin players. When I hear two of these people play the Bach Double slow movement, it sounds to me like a couple of rather under-developed students. A few years ago, before starting a rehearsal of this work, the conductor said to me 'Very lightweight and fast'. I said, 'I'm sorry, I just can't do it like that.' I heard a recent recording of this work, by two very famous violinists who were using that style, without any of the slurs that have been used for the last couple of hundred years. All they managed to do was to make this music sound less expressive.

* * * * *

How was Bach played in the early twentieth century? If you listen to cylinder records of violinists from the turn of the century, you'll hear that there's much less vibrato, and quite a lot more portamento. *Is there any connection with the modern historically informed movement, which largely eliminates vibrato in Bach?* Yes, it does have a connection. Violin playing changed more quickly around 1900 than it had done for the previous hundred and fifty years. It is only in the last century that we have we cultivated the luscious vibrato. In time it brought about this reaction against being so over-expressive.

Recently I went to hear a well-known period orchestra play the Handel Concerto Grosso Op. 6 No.11 in A, which is a great favourite of mine. It has the most wonderful tunes, and I heard them being played with separate bows and no vibrato. For me, it made nonsense of the music. The very musical continuo cellist was making better sense of the music than did the two solo violinists. I've never forgotten that, because it was like somebody playing a theme from the Beethoven or Brahms concerto without vibrato, and all in separate bows. It quite demeaned the music as far as I was concerned.

Casals's Bach was very expressive and rather subjective, but in a universal way. Like it or not, he was able to project a conceptually large vision of the music. But a modern specialist will not agree with this. *They may not agree, but could they totally dismiss it as a human event?* I remember hearing Casals play the Bach C minor Sarabande as an encore at the Queens Hall, just after the war. He made it sound quite wonderful.

There's a lovely contralto aria in the **St. Matthew Passion,** 'Ich barme dich' with a violin obligato. I remember playing it at a concert in the Albert Hall. The gamba player, who was a specialist in old music, said to me 'I find it extraordinary that you're playing this piece totally wrongly, and yet it sounds rather good.' *The word wrongly would have been a judgment based on his assessment of baroque style.* I was using vibrato, for a start. I've always imagined that there were a few talented violinists around in those days who probably could do vibrato; in the same way that there were a few singers who used the modern vibrato. Robert Donnington quotes, in one of his books, a certain singer who was banned from singing on the Cathedral circuit in Italy. This was because of the disturbing, secular way he sang, which had the wrong effect on the congregation. There was no doubt that he was too schmaltzy for them.

An interesting approach to Bach playing of recent times is the use of the baroque violin and bow. In the 1940s and '50s I bought quite a number of transitional and out-curved bows, without slides on the frogs, which nobody wanted in those days. I picked them up from dealers for £5 or £10 a piece—I've still got about twenty of them. I have found that I can play with a good eighteenth-century bow as comfortably as a modern one. The good ones respond excellently. When the baroque revival started, the orchestras didn't have any baroque bows so I lent them mine. I found it very interesting to have young baroque soloists coming here to borrow a bow. Bach, played with an out-curved bow, rather fast and arpeggiated, is nothing like as difficult as when played on a modern violin. If any student of mine wanted to play Bach in the baroque style, I always advised learning first to play the violin really well before deciding which elements of modern technique not to use. *Before the start of the baroque movement there had often been a romantic style superimposed on this music.* I remember Max Rostal talking about this, saying that you wouldn't make the same sound in Bach as in Mozart or Tchaikovsky. He then proceeded to demonstrate, but the the difference in his tone quality wasn't as much as he might have thought. *Even today some people still favour a more romantic approach?* Absolutely, although I think that too romantic an approach is not right for this music.

In exams, I sometimes hear somebody play their couple of Bach movements remarkably well. Later, when playing their romantic concerto, these players tend to be rather lacking in warmth and subtlety in their vibrato; elements in some ways less fundamental for the earlier music.

We cannot be sure how the violin was played in those days, but we do know that the human body was the same shape, although nowadays people are a bit taller. The violin neck was shorter, but thicker. Because of this, players could hang on to the violin a bit better without a shoulder rest, or even a chin rest. The bows that they were using were not very weighty at the top end, and they held them an inch or two up from the nut. They used quite a few more changes of bow—they had to.

* * * * *

There is not just one way to play great music. Providing that the artist has a strong enough personality to be persuasive, it can be played in different tempi and styles. Many different approaches may sound right. Early music players have got as many schisms amongst themselves as early Christians or orthodox Jews. There's a tremendous amount of alleged heresy amongst them. I think it is pretty clear that nowadays the approach to baroque music is already different from the 1970s. At that time, some people pronounced that it had to be a certain way, and that it would be wrong to do it differently. Now it's already changing a bit, but I think that the current approach is far too much bound up with thinking how a work used to be played, rather than where the music is going. The music is far more important than the exact way of playing it.

There are so many different ways of doing things. The first time I played Brandenburg No.3 with just three violins, three violas, three cellos and a bass, was in the late 1940s. I had heard and played this work, with larger forces and a big sound, since I was a schoolboy. Initially this new way seemed frustrating but, with one instrument to a part, I soon began to enjoy the clarity of texture.

When the BBC first started early music broadcasts in 1947, Arnold Goldsborough and Basil Lam were asked to do a lot of performances. When working with them we were asked to start trills on the upper note, on the beat, which was not the way we were used to. I remember Goldsborough saying that if you appreciate a difference in style, you've got to practise it until it works comfortably. While in the process of absorbing this style, I found myself trying upper note trills in the Tchaikovsky Concerto, music of a hundred and seventy years later.

During each month of 1949 we were doing different Bach cantatas. The scoring often included tutti strings, flutes, oboes and trumpets. In one of the cantatas I was thrilled to play the first movement of Brandenburg No. 3 in a wonderful version using full scoring, including wind. This shows how Bach was happy to use alternative scorings in his works. I used to play some of Bach's three part inventions, which Mozart had arranged as string trios, with one adagio in each. His authenticity was only sixty or seventy years out, yet what a terrible modernist Mozart was considered to be in his orchestration of the **Messiah!**

I have heard performances of Mozart piano concertos in which it is obvious that the orchestral material is an urtext edition, because they're playing it with quite different phrasing from the piano soloist. The pianist may be doing wonderful things, while the accompaniment sounds comparatively poker-faced and wooden. *But it doesn't necessarily follow that playing from these editions makes it wooden?* No, but many players, especially students, haven't got the musical background to know what they should put in it—that what is written is only a part of the music. Both Casals and Enescu said that one should learn to play what has not been written down, because only seventy per cent can be notated.

How would you apply that to the unaccompanied violin works of Bach? In Bach slow movements I've always taught my students to begin by playing the tunes, only putting in the extra chords and accompaniments when they get used to the shape of the line. I ask them to make the tunes noble and beautiful, and then to face the challenge of accompanying them without breaking it up into pieces. Unfortunately, in urtext editions (and Galamian's edition of this is based on the urtext), where there is no slur they play separate bows—there are so many places that sound different.

When I was first playing in the Boyd Neel Orchestra, just after the war, we played quite a lot of Handel's **Concerti Grossi**: they were edited for Peter's Edition by Max Sieffert. We always used to cross out a lot of the editor's markings, because he'd put in slurs and crescendos, ornaments and even some small cadenzas. In those days we didn't realise that this was a scholar trying to recreate the performance style of Handel's day. If those editions came out again, they might be considered rather interesting.

Similarly, there was an American edition of the solo Bach works back in the 1940s or '50s by Sol Babitz, a passionate Bach specialist. It is a very free edition, just suggesting what people might have done. There are many musicians who consider that, in Bach's time, they would never have played semiquavers evenly. *We associate that very much with French music.* Yes. *And some say that the principle sometimes applies to Bach's music.* Whenever I was playing French baroque, I would find this really uncomfortable music to play, because there were many types of ornaments and such a different style was asked of us. When Corelli was asked if he would lead the Paris Opera Orchestra, he said that he couldn't do it, because he didn't play in the French style.

David Boyden describes how a member of the musical administration of the King of France went to Italy in the late 1600s to hear the stringed instruments. On his return, he said that they should buy some of these instruments, because of their extra power. When Telemann went to Poland as a guest, he found that the Poles, who were on the outskirts of baroque tradition, were playing about half a tone higher. They played on violins that were a little smaller, and thus shriller. They didn't realise that they were doing some things totally wrongly—according to German tradition.

In the time of Bach, the journey from Hamburg to Frankfurt by coach took a couple of days. You were liable to find a slightly different style in each town—there were many different local styles. Today there's said to be about thirty different sorts of popular music. In my early years I was interested in these fashions, but now I don't know the difference between garage and grunge styles. I find, musically, that rap music is a mystery, because it seems like an accompanied recitative going on for ever, with no actual melody.

A lot of the Bach sonatas were not published till the 1830s. I've got what I think is the earliest printed edition by Ferdinand David, an enthusiastic editor and wonderful fiddle player. He includes both his edited edition and the urtext, as did some later editions. However, he didn't realise that he was using the wrong urtext. The urtext being used in the 1830s was found to be corrupt compared to one discovered later. *The one that we know is considered to be Bach's manuscript?* That's right, yes. *Which is the one that was found in the butcher's shop in Leningrad in 1815?* I forget, but I know that there are certain editings of David that prove that he could never have played some of these works—he was putting in bowings which were impossible. An example of this is when he put two bows per bar in the first movement of the C major Sonata.

Would you say that players should consult various editions to see different possible solutions? Usually young players learning repertoire haven't got the time to be musicologists. I was already well over sixty, and deep into teaching, before I found the pleasure of having two double music stands with four editions of Bach, looking to see how the problems were solved by different players. Occasionally, in a difficult passage, I'd find that a distinguished editor had slipped in a bowing of some description. It proved to me that this person was having some trouble with the original bowings.

Bach is spoken of in Szigeti's little book, **The Violinist's Notebook**, written forty years ago. All the things he's complaining about still exist today. Georg Szell said that when violinists auditioned for his orchestra, they played the big concertos wonderfully for him. They then played the first violin part of a Mozart symphony with no understanding at all.

Twenty years ago, a top violin shop offered for sale a Grancino violin, in totally original condition—what we would call a baroque violin. It was rejected by all the baroque violinists who tried it because, for them, it was too loud. To try to please them, the original bass bar was taken out and a lighter one was put in. Perhaps today, with baroque players having expanded their understanding, that would be considered vandalism. A few years ago, a representative of a major American institution came to show me Corelli's own Amati violin, still in its original state, which he had just bought in an auction. It had been in England for two hundred and fifty years. I played it and was amazed how big the tone was, even with plain gut E and A strings.

It is a good idea to listen to a number of different recordings of Bach by different players, to get an idea of different possibilities. I think the only modern piece written by Bach was the Chaconne, a wonderful virtuoso show-off piece. Perhaps the best performance I've heard of it is by Jascha Heifetz, on one of his seventieth birthday recitals on video. There is some extra ornamentation, put in by his teacher, Leopold Auer. Szigeti said, quite rightly, that one should pay particular attention to Bach and to Paganini, because serious violinists should be working on the problems in these works for their whole career.

Manny Stories

John Batten

A recent photo

Sometimes in ECO rehearsals Manny would quietly make a quizzical or witty remark about what was happening at that moment. While he maintained a calm demeanour, his section would be falling about with laughter.

NONA LIDDELL

MICHAEL HURWITZ

Someone at a summer school was asking Manny a whole series of stupid questions about a piece and was only satisfied when Manny said 'When I discussed this with Carl Flesch, he said to do it this way'. Afterwards I asked him about his meeting with Flesch and he said 'I never actually met him'.

In the early days of giving lessons Manny came into the kitchen looking pleased. He said 'I've just had my first success as a teacher—I've persuaded someone to change to the viola'.

KENNETH ESSEX

The Hurwitz Quartet recorded one of Hindemith's quartets for the BBC. One day at a rehearsal a few weeks later, Manny told his colleagues that, while going round the foreign radio stations late the night before, he had heard a performance of that work; it was so good that he had to listen till the end to find out who was playing. When it was announced as being his own recording, he said that then he realised that it wasn't so good after all.

ADRIAN LEVINE

One day, while I was waiting for my lesson, Manny returned home late after a Philharmonia rehearsal with Klemperer who, he said, was leaning over and looking as if he was going to collapse. Virtually having had to direct the orchestra himself, Manny said wearily 'I'm just a worker bee!'

After one of my early concerts, in which I had played a rather inaccurate Beethoven Romance, Manny said to me 'You know, you're far too young to make so many mistakes!'

Manny mused about a very tall fellow student of mine at the RAM who was having problems, 'It isn't working very well. I wonder if he would do better on the viola, where everything is a bit further away'.

I was playing a Beethoven quartet in Italy which contained a particularly difficult passage. Just before the concert, I was chatting with Manny in the green room. I mentioned this passage and he showed me a fingering which I thought solved the problem. Enthused by this, I attempted it in the concert and made a complete mess of it, ending up doing half the new fingering and half my own. Afterwards, Manny said philosophically, 'You know, you should never change a fingering just before a concert!'

While in Italy on a chamber music course, Manny was about to lead the Mendelssohn Octet, with his Aeolian and my Amphion Quartets, in a local church concert. On the programme also was a local guitarist, scheduled to do a ten minute group of solos. However, this ten minutes grew to twenty, then to thirty and still he went on. He finally wandered off the stage, looking very pleased with himself. In spite of their not having a language in common, Manny, with a sweet smile shook hands and said to him in an artless voice, 'Wonderful playing but too bloody long!'

Then, at the end of the octet, while returning to the platform to acknowledge the applause, Manny noticed that a man near to him in the front row had put a pipe into his mouth. After bowing, Manny looked at him and muttered 'This is the house of God—and you think it's a convenient place for a quiet smoke?'

Just before going on stage with Manny to play the Bach Double, he winked at me and said 'You know, you'll have to fight your corner—I regard a double concerto as a competitive event!'

COLIN CALLOW

When coaching a young Japanese group in the Elgar Quartet, Manny was asked for ideas on how to make it sound English. He replied 'Imagine, in this passage, that a British ship has been holed and is sinking . . . while on deck, the captain is still saluting.'

Manny was asked by a pupil how he managed to keep his violin up. He said 'In 1940 I was playing at a variety show in the Aldershot Hippodrome. It included an act by the stripper Phyllis Dixey, who came out on a plank above the orchestra with just a couple of feather boas. I found that I was always looking upwards; I learnt there both how to hold up the violin and to memorise!'

MARK PTASHNE

One of the regular side events at the Summer School in Italy was the concert in a small town nearby. The audiences were great, hanging from the rafters of the small church, and Manny used to play a Vivaldi concerto. One day things were a bit, shall we say, on the casual side; afterwards Manny said to me backstage 'Now if I were a proper artist I would go upstairs and shoot myself!'

Manny came to a festival in Vermont that I was associated with for some years. He played viola in a quartet I was 'leading'. We did an early Schubert, little rehearsal, too much laughing . . . I remember the question of what to do if you got lost. Manny said he always followed the rule: 'Skip a line or two and pick out a bar; play that bar over and over again until it sounds right and you have found your place.'

* * * * *

KAY HURWITZ

One day, going into a memorial concert of a distinguished colleague, Manny noticed two ladies looking at him with interest. Then one nudged the other and whispered excitedly 'That's the father of Jacqueline Mina!'

JACQUELINE MINA

When we were asked to look after the beloved golden hamster of some friends, Manny felt rather sorry for it having to live in a cage. In his habitual late night photo sessions, he used to release it in his dark room to let it run around a bit. One night it managed to escape from the room and Manny pursued it into the garden, looking under all the bushes to locate it. Eventually he was spotted by a passing policeman, lying on his front lawn, wearing a dressing gown and smoking a cigar. When asked what he was doing, he answered 'Waiting for a hamster'.

Since it did not reappear, he went to great trouble to acquire one that looked identical, in the hope that the friends would not notice. When they returned, he told them enthusiastically how much we had enjoyed housing it. They answered 'Well, that's good because our children seem to have lost interest—so would you like to keep it?'

ELSPETH ILIFF

In 1951, Manny felt very pleased about having learnt to drive. However, referring to the incredibly slow type of weekend motorist, he said 'I don't want to go out on Sundays because the roads are full of mimsers'.

* * * * *

KEITH HARVEY

Sometimes, while driving, Manny liked twiddling the dial around the remote radio stations. He said 'Somewhere there's always a cadenza being played'.

Afternoon rehearsals were never Manny's favourite activity. Towards the end of one, when playing in a chamber group somewhere in the sticks, the erudite pianist was wanting to rehearse every piece in the programme. Finally, Manny looked up at him wearily and said 'This afternoon I'm not looking for greatness!'

There is a violin solo with double stops in the slow movement of Dvorak Symphony No. 4. During a Philharmonia rehearsal in Japan Manny, playing it for the first time, momentarily came to grief, at the same time commenting nonchalantly 'They said it was difficult!'

While I was recording the J.C. Bach **Concertante** with Manny, he got out his cigarettes and lit up rather noisily while I was playing a difficult cello solo passage. When the red light went out, I looked at him enquiringly and he said 'Well, it wasn't any good, was it?'

I did somewhat better in an awkward solo by Alexander Goehr, after which Manny looked over and said 'Would you like to have another go at that sporting event?'

During a long rehearsal of a rather bland piece, Manny said about the rambling middle section 'Nobody's buying, nobody's selling'.

While going through a long-winded and not particularly demanding piece—'Somehow, one's technique always descends to the job in hand'.

About the long and difficult first violin part of the Schubert Octet—'I've discovered a set of fingerings that work well after two hundred miles up the M1'.

During a slightly tense orchestral recording in Germany, Manny diffused the atmosphere by commenting, when there was a rather strange noise offstage, 'I think there's a horse in the bathroom'.

PETER MOUNTAIN

While adjudicating, Manny and I were listening to a girl playing the viola fairly well and musically. The strange thing was that she made an exceptionally small sound. Manny looked at me approvingly and said 'She should be heard!'

NONA LIDDELL

A shy and softly spoken lady violinist, playing in a chamber orchestra, leaned forward to consult Manny about a bowing. Manny answered in a rather quiet voice, winked at her and whispered conspiratorially 'Don't tell anyone!'

KENNETH SILLITO

In my early days in the ECO we were rehearsing a Boccherini symphony with a not overly gifted conductor. He kept talking vaguely about what he wanted and we were going round in circles. After yet another meaningless request, Manny turned to his section and said 'He wants it more like a blancmange'.

After a performance Manny was congratulated by a very famous violinist. He answered 'I'm not a top-class violinist—I just try to sound like one'.

I was playing with Manny and a well-known soloist in a programme featuring Vivaldi concertos for one, two and three violins. In the rehearsal the soloist was having trouble coordinating some intricate filigree passage. Manny whispered to me 'It takes a small man to play small music!'

Many years ago, in a small town bric-a-brac shop, Manny spotted a rather dirty old violin which looked reasonably interesting. The price was ten pounds. Not wanting to spend so much, Manny said to the shopkeeper that he could see the soundpost on the treble side, but that it didn't have one on the other side. The shopkeeper looked a bit concerned and said in that case he could have it for five pounds.

Manny and I were commuting to Cambridge for a few days. One evening, the rehearsal went into extra time and Manny suggested that we stay the night rather than go back. We managed to find a small hotel that had just one twin-bedded room. In the middle of the night I was awakened by a strange swirling sound. Eventually I opened my eyes and looked at my watch which said it was 3.30. Then I looked around me for the source of the sound and saw that Manny was washing his socks!

JØRGEN LAULUND

Just before a Hurwitz Quartet concert in a church, I found that my black bow tie had not been packed. Manny, ever resourceful, hunted in a nearby cupboard till he found an old black cassock. He tore a neat strip off the bottom and tied this for me in an elegant bow.

OTHER CONTRIBUTORS

Terence Weil brought, by mistake, a white tie instead of a black one for a Melos date. This time, Manny improvised by smearing black shoe polish over it. It looked alright from a distance, but was not exactly fragrant.

Rehearsing one day with a distinguished woodwind player, who was accompanying his melody in a rather assertive manner, Manny stopped and said 'I'm very happy to accompany you in your melodies, but I don't want to have to accompany your accompaniment in mine'.

A colleague coming out of a recital at the Wigmore Hall found himself beside Manny who said 'That was extraordinary'. The other said 'I thought it was awful'. Manny said 'Yes, but extraordinarily awful!'

Manny had a solo passage which, to save an awkward page turn, he had written out on two lines and stuck to the top of the page. While getting near this passage, he saw it gradually fall downwards so that it was no longer visible. So he had to play it from memory, which he managed with one wrong note. After the concert, Kay, rather tired after putting their young children to bed said 'Why did you play that wrong note? You woke me up!'

Backstage, after a New York concert in Carnegie Hall, a man strode up to Manny and exclaimed enthusiastically 'Sir, you are a virtuoso page turner!'

While leading a chamber orchestra rehearsal at the Queen Elizabeth Hall, Manny found that the wealthy amateur conductor, who had hired the band for the evening, kept slowing the tempo. He arranged with the distinguished piano soloist that they would just keep going and ignore him. The result was that, in the concert, the conductor periodically stopped beating and then resumed at the orchestra's tempo. The Times review, the following day, praised Manny's management of the difficult situation which, it said, had only a hint of a send-up.

Discography

This is a general guide to the works Manny recorded. Several works, first issued on LP, were later transferred to CD.

L'Oiseau-Lyre
Bach: Sonata in C (with N.Liddell vln, C.Spinks hpsi, T.Weil vcl)
Purcell: 3 Sonatas (with N.Liddell vln, C.Spinks hpsi, T.Weil vcl)
EMI
Shostakovitch: Seven Romances (with G Vishnevskaya sop, M.Rostropovitch vcl, B.Britten pno)

MELOS ENSEMBLE
EMI
Mozart: Clarinet Quintet
Brahms: Clarinet Quintet
Weber: Clarinet Quintet
Reger: Clarinet Quintet (Scherzo only)
Bliss: Clarinet Quintet
Bliss: Oboe Quintet
Beethoven: Septet
Schubert: Octet
Mendelssohn: Octet
Spohr: Double Quartet
Berwald: Grand Septet
Decca
Ravel: Trois Poèmes de Mallarmé (with Janet Baker)
Roussel: Serenade, Delage: Quatres Poèmes Hindous
Ravel: Introduction & Allegro
L'Oiseau-Lyre
Prokofiev: Quintet in G minor
Shostakovitch: Piano Quintet
Schubert: Trout Quintet

Schoenberg: Septet
Schoenberg: Serenade
Sotone
Brahms: Horn Trio
British Music Label
Holbrooke: Piano Quartet in G

HURWITZ CHAMBER ENSEMBLE
L'Oiseau-Lyre
Avison: Concerti 1,2,6,8,9,12 (with I.McMahon vln, C.Spinks hpsi)

ENGLISH CHAMBER ORCHESTRA
Decca
Bach: 6 Brandenberg Concerti (cond B.Britten)
Phillips
Handel: 12 Concerti Grossi (with R.Keenlyside vln, K.Harvey vcl, cond R.Leppard)
EMI
Haydn: Sinfonia Concertante (with K.Harvey, P.Graeme ob, M.Gatt bsn, cond D.Barenboim)
L'Oiseau-Lyre
Mozart: Concertone in C K190 (with E.Goren vln, T.Weil vcl, P.Graeme ob, cond C.Davies)
Lyrita
Holst: Double Concerto (with K.Sillito vln, cond I.Holst)

AEOLIAN QUARTET
Decca
Haydn: complete Quartets, (CD version 22 discs)
Beethoven: the late Quartets: Op. 127, 130, 131, 132, 133, 135
(coupled with Gabrieli Quartet: Op. 18, 59, 74 & 95)
Debussy: Quartet
Ravel: Quartet
Frederic May: Quartet
Mozart: 5 String Quintets

ISBN 0-9544675-0-7

As listeners, when we buy a recording, only the best will satisfy us. Our choice is the one that takes us beyond the notes to the spirit of the music. The path to such achievement is laid out in this book. Whatever your instrument, there is advice on virtuosity, depth of musical understanding and those magical elements that can illuminate a performance.

This is a book for all music students, for young professionals seeking to develop performing and teaching skills and for serious amateurs.

I think that all lovers of music will enjoy this book, not only performers. It's short and always to the point; its 130 pages of stimulating insight are divided into Basics, Homework, Rehearsal, Background, Performance and Post Mortem.

Riki Gerardy has acquired a wealth of knowledge and wisdom about the performance of music from many historical periods. His musical illustrations, drawn from a very broad base, are legible and exceptionally helpful.

HUMPHREY BURTON CBE

Between Music Lessons

How to practise

Riki Gerardy
Zelia 2003
ISBN 0-9544675-1-5

This is a book for every young musician. It will show that you are musical and can express it by playing an instrument well.

Illustrated with lots of cartoons, stories and anecdotes, it reveals how to make practice enjoyable. Learn technical skills and every aspect of musicality.

This is a preliminary volume to Beyond the Music Lesson, a handbook for advanced students.

> Between Music Lessons *is intended for children. It is entertainingly illustrated in the style of the cartoonist Mel Calman and is full of practical advice for young students of any instrument, from their earliest days onwards. (I enjoyed it a lot and I've just turned seventy.)*
>
> *The style is direct, the sentences short and pithy. The subject matter is how music works—the very stuff of music itself!*
>
> HUMPHREY BURTON CBE